The Pride and The Shame of a Coalminer's Bairns

Poppy Whitfield

authorHOUSE®

AuthorHouse™ UK
1663 Liberty Drive
Bloomington, IN 47403 USA
www.authorhouse.co.uk
Phone: 0800.197.4150

Published by AuthorHouse 12/03/2014

ISBN: 978-1-4969-9805-7 (sc)
ISBN: 978-1-4969-9800-2 (hc)
ISBN: 978-1-4969-9806-4 (e)

Library of Congress Control Number: 2014921346

If you are reading this then it means I have finally done what my dear friend Murphy has always encouraged me to do and that is to write a book about my childhood so here goes ...

Chapter 1

The Village

My story began way back in a small coal mining village in the North-East of England which can be traced back for up to one thousand years. The unusual name of the village derives from two Anglo-Saxon words which spelt together 'Heppedune' or Bramble Hill. History has it that a local landowning family called the Le Hepdons owned part of an ancient Manor which was bounded by that of Elemore and divided into two parts. During this time life in the village and estates was one of self-sufficiency and contact with the outside world was limited due to difficulties accessing the village because of the poor tracks. This was way back in the days where the horse and cart were relied upon for transport.

Firstly I'd like to tell you a little bit about my family and where my story originally began; so let me give you a little background information about my Parents and how they came to meet. My Dad was the youngest boy of eight children, three boys Bobby and Jesse and five girls Marjorie, Maureen, Beryl, Kitty and Jean who unfortunately died when she was a baby before my

Dad was even born. Now let me tell you the story of how Dad got his name. Immediately following Dad's birth the midwife asked my Grandma Myrtle if she had decided on a name for her new-born and as the answer was no the Midwife said that some friends of hers who were living close by had by pure coincidence the same surname as my family had lost their only Son in the Battle of Britain, she went on to tell my Grandma that their Son was a Fighter Pilot who was unfortunately killed whilst serving his King and Country. The Midwife wondered if my Grandma would consider naming her baby after the Pilot. Dad as it happens has told me his version of the story but added that there is a Memorial dedicated to the young Pilot in the local Cemetery which pays tribute to his namesake.

My Mam Alice was the middle child of five, two boys Edgar Jnr and Jack and three girls, Margaret who was the eldest and was named after my Granda Edgar's only sister and May who was the baby of the five and was named after her maternal Grandma, I think that my Mams name came from Grandma too, their parents were Edgar and Greta.

The good thing about my family is that we are big, Dad being one of eight children and Mam being one of five which resulted in the birth of nine Paternal Grandchildren and nineteen Maternal Grandchildren of whom the list of relatives to this day is ever expanding, On the downside though our surname ends with my Brother but lives on through my Son who I feel proud to have had it included as his middle name.

My Dad was 15 years old when he left School and became a Coal Miner at the local Colliery. He eventually worked his way up to becoming a Hewer which meant that he was responsible for cutting the coal and removing it from the coal face. His job was one of the most dangerous jobs in the mine as coal would fall from the face and sometimes the roof would fall in. Hewing was hard work and the mining culture in many places recorded the strength and bravery of the Hewer. I always had this preconceived idea that Dad would have hated working down the

Pit but when I asked him about his job as a Miner he surprised me by telling me that he absolutely loved it. I think one of the reasons he loved it was because of the camaraderie and as such it is often said that anyone with connections to the village has coal dust running through their veins. Dad told my Brother that on his very first day of work he went downstairs ready to leave to do his very first shift at the Pit when my Granda Gilbert presented him with a full English breakfast and Dad responded by saying "Thanks but I don't want anything to eat". Granda then apparently said to Dad "No child of mine leaves this house to do a full day's work without having a good breakfast inside them". My Brother said that after a few years of working at the Pit he made the decision to transfer to another Pit which was over two hundred miles away in Staffordshire and on his first morning in his new job Dad felt this overwhelming feeling of homesickness particularly as he missed having his breakfast with his Da.

I recently discovered that my Dad was originally offered a position with the Co-operative Butchers in the village before leaving school but apparently the Headmaster of the School was very strict and refused to give Dad a reference. It wasn't because Dad was a bad lad or anything like that; he was just one of the gang, so to speak. He was never in trouble because he just wasn't that kind of lad, infact my Auntie Marjorie said that the situation could have been easily rectified if Grandma and Granda had gone into the school to discuss the matter further. I on the other hand am a firm believer that everything happens for a reason and this was not meant to be.

Both of my Dad's Parents were very quiet natured and my Auntie Beryl fondly recalls the time when her and my Uncle Jesse were fighting with one another on the staircase, My Grandma just happened to be in the Hallway on her hands and knees polishing all the shoes when the fight got out of hand and my Grandma threw a shoe brush at both of them to try and put an end to the argument but it hit Auntie Beryl on the back of her knee and made her leg bleed. This reaction totally shocked both children as they cannot remember ever being smacked by either of their Parents. My Auntie Beryl also said that my Grandma never ever left the house but this didn't mean that their house was ever quiet or empty; it was just the opposite as it was a popular place for visitors to call by and have a cup of tea and a chat with her.

My Mam was fortunate enough to attend the local Grammar School, I say fortunate as children were classed as being very privileged if they were selected as firstly they had to pass the 11+ Entrance Exams before they were even considered to be offered a place. The 11+ was introduced in the UK in 1944 and was a general test of intelligence, it tested a Student's ability to solve problems using Verbal Reasoning and Mathematics and was offered to some Students in the last year of Primary education which then governed various types of Secondary education appropriate to the Child's ability. Once Mam had completed her education she secured a position as an Office Clerk with a Company which I think was based in Sunderland. I can't tell you anything more about her role, other than she travelled to and from work on the local bus and on one of her daily commutes she had some kind of 'funny do' on the bus which she blamed on after eating a banana, She said that the banana had caused her to experience her first 'to do' with her heart which I shall tell you about in a little while. As it happens, bananas are something that I believe she has never eaten since that day.

My Parents met at about the age of fourteen. Soon after my Mam and family *flitted from another village close by to the village where my Dad and his family lived, infact, they moved into the terraced house next door to my Dad which happened to be only two bedroomed. It must have been a hard decision for my Maternal Grandparents to make as the house that they chose to leave was brand new and had an inside bathroom which was a real luxury compared to the old terraced house

---

* Flitted – Geordie word for moved house.

as this was a basic two up two down with an outside *Nettie. The only reason they moved was because the terraced house was a Colliery house and therefore the rent was free as it was attached to my Granda Edgar's salary.

My Auntie May said that my Mam, who was fifteen at the time, shared a bedroom with her and their Brother Jack which must have been difficult. It was, apparently, at this house that my Grandma Greta's fear of being locked in confined areas came to the surface after she got herself locked inside the outside nettie and by all accounts was in there for quite a few hours, Once released she was in a right old state vowing from that day forward to never lock the door on a toilet again even if it was a public one preferring instead to secure the door from the inside by wedging her handbag up against the bottom of the door. A few years passed by and my Parents made the decision to get engaged and it wasn't long after that Mam flitted again with her family to a coal mining town in Staffordshire as her Da had been offered a job in a Pit down there. Soon afterwards Dad decided to follow her and take advantage of a job opportunity with the Pit which included a brand new Colliery house in the next village which was just a bus ride away from the rest of the family who had by now already settled down. It must have been hard for Dad to leave his family and make the move but I guess love makes you brave and bold and he must have been sure that everything was going to work out just fine. If only he could have seen into the future he would have seen that his dream would be shattered. You see the tragic thing about my story is time ... this isn't a story where boy meets girl and they fall in love, get married, have two kids and live in a house with roses around the door, No! this story is about a dream that is shattered piece by piece over a long, very painful period of time, a time that eventually ate into the decades of all our lives and claimed an enormous piece of us all to the point where we are left still trying to piece together certain events in our lives.

---

* Nettie – Geordie word for Lavatory.

My Parents eventually married, Dad was 20 and Mam was 19, so in effect Dad married the girl next door, apparently they used to knock on the dividing bedroom wall to one another using some sort of code. They married in May 1964, Dad looked very handsome on his wedding photographs, wearing a grey suit, white shirt and skinny tie with his hair slicked back with a 'kiss curl' similar to Elvis Presley's. He looked utterly dashing if I do say so myself and they looked perfect together and made a very handsome couple. When some years later my friends saw the black and white wedding photographs they nervously laughed and said that Mam looked like Myra Hindley, I guess in hind sight this did not bode well! Their Wedding made the local news with the following article:

Bride and Groom were sent to Warwickshire – for a Honeymoon – by their Friends, following their marriage on Saturday. They were Alice Daughter of Edgar and Greta and (My Dad) Son of Gilbert and Myrtle of Co. Durham who were married at the Central Methodist Church.

The Bride is a Clerk and the Groom is a transferred Miner from Durham.

The Bride wore a full-length, long-sleeved, white lace dress with a white nylon train.

The Bridesmaids were Misses May (Brides Sister), Lindsay and Clare (Brides Nieces) and Miss Carol B*******.

The Best Man was Mr Keith W******. A reception for 70 Guests was held in the Mining Youth Centre in the town.

Myra Hindley for those of you who do not know was an English Serial Killer during the 1960's who in partnership with her Boyfriend Ian Brady committed the rapes and murders of five small children. Hindley's 17 year old Brother-in-Law tipped her off to the Police and when she was arrested she pleaded not guilty to all of the murders. She was found guilty of three murders and was jailed for life and died in prison in 2002.

Anyway back to the story ... my Parents soon settled down to married life and my Brother Kelvin was born thirteen months later at the local Hospital in June 1965. Both Mam and him had a rather traumatic time which apparently had nothing to do with him being a big baby weighing in at 8lb odd. Mam said that he was what they called a Blue baby which was due to the Umbilical Cord being wrapped tightly around his neck. Now if only we had been twins I might have been tempted to tamper with his Umbilical Cord, for reasons you will fully understand when I explain about our relationship later on. In August 1967 my Parents eagerly awaited my arrival and Mam was not so keen on repeating the experience that she had when she had given birth to my Brother so instead she opted for a more relaxed home birth. I followed by way of a less traumatic home birth at the beginning of August weighing in at either 7lb 3ozs or 7lb 7ozs. The Midwife who delivered me was apparently 84 years old and I was born to the sound of Big Ben chiming on the ten o'clock news. In the meantime Dad waited patiently downstairs for my arrival. I am told that when I was born I had just a tiny little spot of blood on my nose and therefore did not need any cleaning up as such. Mam said that my birth was a *doddle and she made a quick recovery afterwards. Dad got into trouble with Mam when she later discovered that he had accidentally caught the shiny fender on the open fire when he was attempting to burn the afterbirth. She was so houseproud and this small thing was a big deal to her.

Elvis Presley topped the charts with "Crying in the Chapel" the week that Kelvin was born and "All you need is Love" by the Beatles hit number 1 when I arrived.

Dad used to say that I used to frighten the life out of him most days when I was a baby because when either of my Parents

---

* Doddle – Geordie word for easy.

used to put me outside in the garden in my pram for fresh air I would just sleep the day away to the point where by the time I had missed three feeds he would come and check on me to see if I was still breathing. He used to spend hours and hours pushing firstly my Brother and then me in our pram for miles and miles. He reckons even then that Mam was a big 'show off' as he said that she had to choose the biggest pram in the shop which he found was bloody murder to manoeuvre particularly in and out of doorways and up and down steps. Dad pushed all the babies in the family and his technique made me laugh as he used only one hand to both steer and secure the pram.

I guess it wasn't cool in those days for men to be seen with both hands on the handlebars or maybe it was because he would be pushing the pram with one hand and trying to hold onto my rebel of a Brother with the other hand! Hmm, my Brother, Dad always used to laugh about Kelvin and his antics especially when we moved again to be closer to our family. There was just no way of containing my Brother and because of this our Parents paid for a private contractor to fence our corner plot garden in the hope that they could contain him but Kelvin had other ideas and when they weren't looking he used to pull his tin pedal car up against the fence and climb onto it and use it as a step for the "Great Escape" to our Maternal Grandparents house which was just in the next street and if you think that is bad, it was nothing compared to what he did another time ... he drank a whole bottle of creamy pink Windolene and Mam and Dad had to rush him to the Doctors or Hospital where they were advised to flush the chemicals out of his system by giving him lots of fresh milk to drink. Dad said that the little shite shit on every step of the staircase and the clean-up operation was not only horrendous but never ending! I loved to hear Dad say shite! He said it with such emotion it was funny to hear.

I would like to say that before we get into the story too much I would like to point out that at this stage of my Mam's life she was a very popular member of the family and as such everyone loved spending time with her, she was intelligent and a fun person to be around and I think that because she was the life and soul of the party, people loved being in her company and as such we had many visitors to our house including Mam's baby Sister May and youngest Brother Jack. Everyone always had such a good time when they came to see us and it was great for us to remain close to our families. God only knows what happened to Mam but something in her was triggered and she wasn't the same person again. I'm not sure if the badness was always in her or if something happened and it was plain madness either way it is a question I doubt I will ever truly unearth the answer to.

Just before we continue I mentioned earlier a little bit of history about the village in the North-East and I am left wondering if any of you have heard of it before? Maybe some of you have heard the Bowes-Lyon name. You will be familiar with the name if you have a keen interest in the Royal Family as a descendant of the Owners of the local Mine was eventually to marry our future King, that person was Elizabeth Angela Marguerite Bowes-Lyon better known as the Queen Mother, she was the ninth of ten children to Claude Bowes-Lyon, 14th Earl of Strathmore and Kinghome, and Cecilia Cavendish-Bentinck who was the Daughter of a Vicar and the descendant of the Dukes of Portland. Four years after her birth, Elizabeth's parents became Lord and Lady Strathmore and remained somewhat impoverished for most, if not all of their lives. The Bowes part of the name came from a marriage with the heiress of the County Durham family of Bowes.

Elizabeth later married Prince Albert who she lovingly referred to as Bertie; he was the Duke of York and second Son of King George V and Queen Mary. They were blessed with two children Queen Elizabeth II and Princess Margaret, Countess of Snowdon. The Queen Mother became fondly known by the nation as the 'Smiling Duchess' because of her consistent public expression, her Husband unexpectedly became King (George VI) when his Brother Edward VII abdicated in order to marry an American divorcee called Wallis Simpson. Now as a

British Monarch this put Edward in an awkward position as he was the nominal head of the Church of England which did not allow people to remarry if their ex-spouses were still alive and Wallis was an American Socialite who was not only divorced from her first Husband but was also pursuing a divorce from her second Husband. Edward abdicated in December 1936 and he remains the only British Monarch to have voluntarily renounced the throne since the Anglo-Saxon period, he was given the title His Royal Highness the Duke of Windsor and married Wallis the year after. They remained married for a further 35 years until his death.

More recently the village attracted the Media through the marriage of Prince William of Wales and Catherine Elizabeth 'Kate' Middleton. This union drove my Dad *crackers because the Film Crews and Journalists that were swarming the village were making the place look like it was a real dump. Dad said it was a bloody farce ... he was really annoyed because all the scenes that were televised were the worst scenes you could have looked at. He wanted to know why they hadn't filmed the beautiful Country Park instead of making the place look like a bloody dump. Part of the filming was shot in Market Street and showed a real poor example of the area due to them focussing on a really rough looking gable end of a house that was covered in graffiti and was quite clearly in a state of disrepair.

If we go further back in history I can tell you the story of two girls who were both born in 1819 but led very different lives from one another – Alexandrina Victoria Guelph and Martha Stephenson. The first was born in Kensington Palace and was later to be crowned Queen Victoria and the second was born on Wearside married a Miner and worked as a Washerwoman. Almost two centuries on Mrs Stephenson's Great-great-great-great Granddaughter is our future Queen. Kate Middleton's Great-Grandfather Thomas Harrison was the Son of a Miner at

---

* Crackers – Geordie word for annoyed.

the same Pit that my Dad first went to work in and he was born June 23rd 1904 and brought up in the same village and later lived at several addresses in the village which were all Colliery houses. Thomas broke several generations of family traditions of mining by becoming a Carpenter and eventually moved his family to London. The Harrison family history began in the village in 1821 when Kate's great-great-great-great Grandfather James who was born in 1796 moved the fifteen miles with his Wife Jane from Byker in Newcastle-upon-Tyne with their family to begin working at another Colliery when it first opened. Unfortunately, James later lost his wife at the age of about 49 years old to an outbreak of Cholera which ravished the North-East and claimed the lives of about 31,000 people. Cholera is a dreadful epidemic to contend with largely because it is unseen. It was a major problem from 1831 for at least 50 years and first arrived in Sunderland and then London almost simultaneously and spread rapidly. Both National and Local Government were forced to do something about the public water services and general sanitation levels but things were not really actioned with any vigour until about the 1840's.

It has also been suggested that the Harrison's will have known Mary Ann Cotton who was one of the most notorious Murderers of the 19th Century. Infact, she was Britain's first Serial Killer and her method was to poison her victims with Arsenic. She was born Mary Ann Robson on the 31st October in 1832 in a small village near to my family's village, her Father Michael was a Pitman who was later killed in 1842 when Mary Ann was only 9 years old, apparently, he fell to his death down a mine shaft while trying to repair a pulley wheel. It is thought that Mary Ann killed as many as twenty one victims – eight of her own Children, seven Step-children, her Mother, three Husbands, a Lover and a Friend. What was her motive? She disguised her motive by living for a short while with her new Husbands before poisoning them and any of their children. Afterwards she would claim their estates by way of cashing in their insurance policies.

When Mary Ann was finally arrested her trial was delayed until the birth of her last child, a girl, who was born inside Durham Gaol. Afterwards Mary Ann was executed by means of hanging at the Gaol on the 24th March 1873 and her remains are buried in the Prison Grounds. Her hanging was botched as the drop below the trap door was too short and she was left jerking on the end of the rope. Hangman William Calcraft had to press down on her to finish the job off and since then she had her own rhyme after her hanging:

Mary Ann Cotton, she's dead and rotten, lying in a bed with her eyes wide open Sing, Sing. What song should I sing? Mary Ann Cotton is tied up with string Where? Where? She's up in the air, and they're selling puddens a penny a pair.

As a matter of interest the following Sports personalities are also from the village: the former Footballers Alan Ball who is now Honorary Director of Queen of the South Football Club, Ralph Coates who played for Burnley and Tottenham Hotspurs, Bob Paisley who was Manager of Liverpool Football Club, Harry Potts who was Manager of Burnley Football Club and Bryan 'Pops' Robson former Footballer of Sunderland United and Newcastle United Football Clubs. In August 2008 the people of the village unveiled a fantastic Memorial to Bob Paisley before Liverpool's opening day win at Sunderland. The Memorial is in the town's main park very close to the old Colliery pitch where Bob played as a Lad. Music fame came from Trevor Horn CBE, a Record Producer, Songwriter, Musician and Singer who also originates from there. Trevor's influence in the 1980's was such that he has been called "The Man Who Invented the Eighties" and he also won a Grammy Award for producing "Kiss from a Rose" by Seal and as a Musician had Chart success with the bands The Buggles, Yes and Art of Noise. As it happens the first vinyl single that Mam bought for me was "Video killed the Radio Star" by the Buggles which I have to say was not my choice but was released in 1979 and was a huge success.

Chapter 2

Everyday –
(Buddy Holly)

I have gone off track a little so let's get back to the village for a little taste of what life was like in the village where most people were born, bred and died having never moved away. Infact it was common practice for a Neighbour to be called in to deliver a baby or to 'lay out' the dead. The 'laying out' of the body or 'rendering the last offices' was traditionally carried out by women, very often the local Midwife. The body was undressed, washed and all orifices plugged. Eyes would be closed and if they would not stay closed then traditionally an old penny was placed upon each eyelid. A bandage would be placed beneath the chin in order to encourage the mouth to remain closed. Once this process was completed the body could then be dressed in its burial clothes and prepared for the coffin by holding limbs straight with bandages or ribbons wrapped around the body at the elbows, wrists and ankles, sometimes thread would be put around the big toes. The coffin would then be placed in the best room of the house 'the Parlour' which was only used on a Sunday or for special occasions or for receiving Visitors to the house. Here the coffin would stay until the day of the funeral as it gave friends and family the opportunity to pay their last respects to their loved one.

The houses where both of my families lived had outside Netties in the back yard which I mentioned earlier and a tin bath which was set in front of the fire at bath time. The bath would be hung on a nail on the yard wall when it was not in use. The houses were situated back to back so each yard would face one another. Each property had a very small carbon footprint in comparison to today but back then it didn't seem to matter as Siblings used to share beds, bedrooms, toys and clothes and it was quite common for Newlyweds to start married life living with the in-laws while they waited for a Colliery house to become vacant or until they had saved up for a while before moving into a place of their own. I have no idea how everyone fitted into these tiny houses but they managed it somehow. Most families relied heavily on growing their own vegetables in their allotments as this would help to stretch the family income. If you still lived at home you would be expected to *'tip up' most of your wages to your Parents as it would be included as part of the household income.

Monday was traditionally wash day which by all accounts was extremely hard work. Out would come the old dolly tub and mangle, wooden dolly pegs would secure the clean washing to the washing lines which would be stretched across the back alleyways which backed the houses. Tuesday would be ironing day and this was another laborious chore as there were no *swanky gadgets in those days. The iron was extremely heavy and was heated up on the Range.

During this time life was hard and the Pit was all about making profits, therefore not many Mine Owners were considered to

---

* Tip Up - Geordie name for hand over.

* Swanky - Geordie name for posh.

be good Employers. Infact the moment a Miner was injured or killed in a Pit accident their families would be swiftly evicted from their homes onto the street where they had nowhere to go; this is why most families had lots of Children as they tended to follow their Father into the Pit and if a disaster were to happen then the families were less likely to lose their home. The reality of this dilemma was that if a family failed to secure employment quickly then some families ended up in the Workhouse as the only other choice would be to starve on the street. So many families had little or no choice and would therefore make the extremely harsh decision of going into the Workhouse.

In Victorian times children were expected to work too and they would start work as early as 4 years old, some pushed trucks of coal along the underground tunnels and were called 'Putters' and some opened and shut wooden doors to let air through the tunnels and these were called 'Trappers'. Trapper boys sat in the dark with just a small candle for light and they had no-one to talk to. Some children started work at 2am and stayed below ground for an incredible eighteen hours while some were lucky enough to work on the surface sorting coal where at least they had daylight and fresh air. It is so hard to imagine what life must have been for the children as I couldn't imagine my Son starting work at 4 years old let alone completing an eighteen hour shift day in day out. They had little choice though as this was the difference between eating and starving to death.

The main family meal of the day was dinner and it was served at lunchtime rather than in the evening. The lighter evening meal was referred to as tea and was served around 6pm. Supper was served immediately before bedtime and could be anything from a glass of milk, bowl of cereal, bread and butter or bread and beef dripping. Personally I preferred toasted crumpets with lashing of best butter melting into them. Meat usually came from two sources, the local Butchers as did the eggs, suet and curds and from Rabbiting which was the sport of hunting rabbits usually Cottontails, often using Ferrets or

Dogs which would track the prey and then various trapping and shooting methods would be used to catch them. Roast dinner on a Sunday was the biggest dinner of the week with the gigantic Yorkshire Puddings served with gravy separately prior to the meat which tended to either be beef or chicken. There were always at least three types of vegetables served with the main course. Offal was another main ingredient of family meals with Liver and Spanish onions being one of the old favourites which I hated as I could not stand the texture of the Liver. Kidneys and Stewing Steak made pies. Tripe which I believe was another cheap food and one that gladly never featured on our dinner table, or Savoury Dumplings which my Mam made and were blinking awful as they were soggy and slimy and cooked by floating on the top of a soup or broth. Most Friday dinners were of Fish from the local Wet Fish shop usually Cod or Smoked Haddock which were then poached in milk and cooked in the oven and served with potatoes of some kind. Christians traditionally eat fish on Fridays because in ancient times meat was a luxury and fish and vegetables were cheaper and more available and both Fridays and Wednesdays were the days set out for fasting. Friday was chosen because it was the day that Jesus was crucified and Wednesday because it was the day that Judas betrayed Jesus.

As you can see from this very brief bit of information life was a lot harder than it is today and in the 50's or 60's Health Care was a lot different too, for example, a Woman probably knew that she was Pregnant before any tests were done as there was no such thing as a Home Pregnancy Test. We really are spoilt today as these are readily available to buy over the Counter in most Retail Outlets. After attending an appointment with the Family Doctor a urine sample would be sent to the Laboratory where it would be injected into a rabbit. If the rabbit lived the test was negative and if the rabbit died this was deemed as a positive test for pregnancy. The words "pregnancy or pregnant" were not spoken about in public, instead the Woman was "with child", "in the family way" or "expecting". No one suggested that you refrain from smoking or drinking alcohol, infact while you were waiting for your appointment to see your Doctor you could smoke in the Waiting Room and once you were in with your Doctor he or she would offer you a light for your cigarette.

Pregnant women did not attend Funerals due to superstitious reasons and once home the baby would not be allowed out of the house until it had been Baptised and when a Woman went into labour she did it without her Husband or Family being present and they were not allowed to see the Patient until both her and the Baby had been cleaned up.

Most people smoked and people could smoke while they were in their hospital bed with ashtrays being provided by the Hospital. At the same time Breast was considered to be not best and Bottle feeding was encouraged. The baby only came to the Mother from the Nursery when it was feeding time and returned there immediately afterwards, only Mother and baby were allowed in the room at feeding times.

It was rare for families not to rent or own a Black and White Television and as such entertainment at home would either be the TV or the Wireless (Radio), I'm not sure of the names of any other rental companies apart from Radio Rentals but there must have been lots as having a television was classed as being swanky and so too was having a motor car. Tongues would wag with envy when someone in the same street as you beat you to it and became the first person to have either of these luxuries. In the 1960's the streets were much safer than they are today with fewer vehicles and because of this children could play out in the street to the usual games such as skipping, football and cricket as well as a variety of other games. Local Dances and Cinema trips were high on the list for adult entertainment along with watching local Bands or the local Football Team along with Day Trips out to Seaton Carew and Finchale Abbey where the family would take a picnic and spend a Sunday away from the home. Seaton Carew is a small seaside resort near to Hartlepool and is named after a Norman

French family called Carou who owned land there and settled there, the 'Seaton' means Farmstead or Settlement by the Sea.

Finchale Priory sometimes referred to as Finchale Abbey was a 13th Century Benedictine Priory sited by the River Wear and served at one point as a Holiday Retreat to the Monks from Durham Cathedral. The site can be reached from Durham via a beautiful riverside and woodland walk and both sides of my families have mentioned happy days out to both of these places.

Personally, it has always been my intention to visit the Open Air Museum located at Beamish near the town of Stanley, County Durham, this is the place to go and take a peek of what life was like back in the olden days. The Museum's principal is to preserve an example of everyday life in Urban and Rural North-East England at the climax of the Industrialisation in the early 20th Century. Beamish opened in 1972 and is situated on 300 acres of land and one of the things that it has managed to recreate is its own Pit Village which is set in the early 1900's, a golden era for the North-East Coal Industry and where free Colliery houses and a generous coal allowances were provided to the Miners, infact, Francis Street which is a traditional terraced row of Miners' Cottages from the village were taken down brick by brick and re-built at Beamish. Also the 102 year old Silver Band Hall which was originally in Market Street has also been moved to Beamish where it has been brought back to life again with the sound of brass band music. Speaking of Brass Bands brings back another memory of my Dad. His favourite *fillem, well he had two favourites to be fair, one being the 1996 British Comedy Drama film "Brassed Off" written and directed by Mark Herman and starring Pete Postlesthwaite, Tara Fitzgerald and Ewan McGregor and is about the troubles faced by a Colliery Brass Band, following the closure of their Pit and it's simply brilliant! The other film is The Shawshank Redemption 1994 American drama film written and directed

---

* Fillem - Geordie word for films.

by Frank Darabont and starring Tim Robbins and Morgan Freeman. The film was adapted from a Stephen King book and tells the story of a Banker who is sentenced to 19 years in the Shawshank State Prison for the murder of his unfaithful Wife and her Lover. It is also one of my personal favourites and I cannot help wondering if Dad on a few occasions had likened himself to the Banker and maybe his dream would have been to carry out a similar crime against my Mam or maybe that is wishful thinking ... Either way I don't think Mam was worth my Dad's freedom being taken away from him.

The last film I watched with Dad was with my Son when we were visiting the North-East, he had bought me the 2009 film Inglorious Basterds for Mother's Day and we sat in what Dad called the "Cowboy Room" which was the second Reception room of his Dormer Bungalow and where he loved to watch all of his Cowboy and War films. Anyway the film is a German-American black comedy war film written and directed by Quentin Tarantino and starring Brad Pitt and it's based on two plots to assassinate Nazi Germany's political leadership. The film that I remember the most was when Dad took both Kelvin and me to the Cinema in 1975 (Pictures as he called it) to watch the American Thriller "Jaws" which was directed by Steven Spielberg and for those of you who are not familiar with the film it was about a giant man-eating Great White Shark that terrorised the summer resort of Amity Island. It left me totally terrified to the point that my head was buried into Dad's chest for most of the movie, particularly the scene where a human head emerges from a sunken vessel. It made Dad jump out of his skin, snapping his black leather belt clean in two in the process. Of course, my Brother wasn't scared at all ... Show off! Jaws as it happens was the highest-grossing film in history at the time, and was the most successful motion picture of all time until Star Wars.

A lot of good times were shared by the three of us including Day Trips out to visit various places in the North-East one being our old favourite which was in Durham City itself. We always used to visit 'The Cathedral Church of Christ, Blessed Mary the Virgin and St. Cuthbert of Durham (Durham Cathedral). When we toured the Cathedral we would opt for the extremely strenuous task of climbing the 325 steps to the top of the Tower and it was on one of these trips that Dad told me and my Brother that on one of his previous visits he had seen Myra Hindley in the Exercise Yard of the Prison Ground, I think that this story was due to the fact that the Tower overlooks the Prison. I have serious doubts about this story being true as Dad must have had extremely good eyesight to have seen anyone from that distance let alone the face of Myra Hindley, nevertheless it's one of the stories that I love and one that I wouldn't change for the world. The views are magnificent from the top of the Tower and on a clear day you can see 'The Angel of the North' which is a contemporary sculpture designed by Antony Gormley and is located in Gateshead and faces the Cathedral and cost a massive £1,000,000. We also used to enjoy a walk along the River Wear and then lunch in a Café that served the most amazing Fish and Chips. Dad continued the tradition with his Grandson by taking him to Durham where they would visit the Cathedral and Durham Light Infantry Museum and on some of these occasions we have also hired a Rowing Boat to take a closer look at the wildlife on the river. A tour of Durham Castle and University has always been an interesting one no matter how many times we have participated, as the stories of Ghosts seem to hold the attention of all the Visitors and my Son in particular was interested in the Armoury that is displayed upon the ancient walls. In the Market Place stands the statue of the 3rd Marquess of Londonderry (Charles William Vane Tempest Stewart) which was unveiled in 1861. He owned many of the Coal Mines in County Durham and invested a lot of money trying to improve the Mines by trying to help them to run better and he also commissioned the building of Seaham Harbour which as it happens was one of my Dad's favourite places and which he used to enjoy to visit most days. Legend has it that the Sculptor Signor Raphael Monti boasted that no one would be able to find fault with his statue of the 3rd Marquess until one day a blind man pointed out that the horse did not have a tongue after he felt inside the horse's mouth. This story has been told to me many times and Dad continued the tradition with not only his Grandson but the other youngsters in our family, none of us guessed the flaw by the way.

More recently in May of this year the 'Mail Online' reported the following local story:

Sculpture of British Tommy reflecting upon the horrors of World War One during the first minute after peace was declared installed for Centenary.

A war-weary Tommy sits thoughtfully, head bowed, rifle in hand, as he reflects upon the sheer horror of World War One during the first minute after peace was declared in 1918.

This imposing metal sculpture, entitled 1101, owing to the fact the armistice went into effect at 11am on November 11, 1918, stands 9ft 5ins tall and weighs 1.2 tonnes.

Built out of special corteen steel, it has been installed on Seaham seafront in County Durham to mark the Centenary of the start of the Great War and will remain in place for three months.

Created by local Artist Ray Lonsdale, the sculpture is also intended to represent Post Traumatic Stress Disorder which many of the returning Soldiers endured. Mr Lonsdale got his idea for the piece after hearing a story about a Soldier from nearby Murton who won a war medal.

A poem by the Artist is inscribed on the side of the sculpture.

NOW ADRIFT IN THE WAKE OF THIS
GLORIOUS SLAUGHTER,
HE'D SEEN MANY A SOUL CLEANSED IN FILTHY WATER.

SEEN GODLESS MEN REACH OUT FOR THE BIBLE,

AS LEAD TORE THE FLESH FROM
BOTH FRIEND AND RIVAL.
SOON HOME TO THE JOY AND CELEBRATION OF KIN,
DRUNKEN SLAPS ON THE BACK AT A FAVOURITE INN.

BUT HEAVY IN HIS POCKET LIES A SMALL PIECE OF CARD,
AND THE NOTE WRITTEN ON IT WILL
BREAK A MOTHERS HEART.

ELEVEN 'O' ONE

I love 'Tommy' and can honestly say that I think it is the most amazing sculpture I have ever seen and I am sure my Dad would think the same.

CHAPTER 3

Shakespeare Avenue

Now I can tell you where I come into the story by explaining to you about my earliest memory, I think this is important as the story is from my point of view. However, my Brother has helped me out along the way particularly when I have felt the need for some clarification regarding certain events. I also feel that I should point out to you that this is from my memory and therefore because I was so young it may vary slightly from my Brother's version of events however I would like to assure you that this book is totally true and I would like to invite you to take this journey back with me to the earlier years of my life.

I remember sitting in a portable swing that was fixed by two hooks to the frame of the side door of a pebble dashed house in Shakespeare Avenue and my Mam pushing me intermittently as she got on with the housework. Our door faced the neighbour's door and if my memory serves me well I think a lovely Scottish couple called Elena and Isaac lived there. Our other next door neighbours were a huge Irish family, the Father Paddy (Patrick) was a total brute and I don't say that lightly, amazingly enough he was married to a lovely woman and they had about four kids one of which was Patrick Jnr, a Daughter that I can't remember the name of, and two other kids. Basically all the neighbours hated Paddy as he was a troublemaker; they got really sick of all the trouble he was constantly creating. One Friday or Saturday night things got out of hand and a fight broke out in the street which involved Paddy, the neighbours and Dad. Somewhere along the line Isaac also got involved in the altercation which sadly ended when Paddy was stabbed and Isaac arrested. During the Trial the Judge although lenient with Isaac still sentenced him to a spell in Prison. On hearing the outcome of the trial all the Villagers were astounded and in uproar and because of this it became too difficult for us to live next door to Paddy and his family so we left Shakespeare Avenue and moved to a house in a cul-de-sac on the other side of the village.

It was while we were still living in Shakespeare Avenue that I remember a white Canary or Cockatoo that Mam used to put out on top of the concrete coal bunker in the back garden supposedly for fresh air until one day the bird mysteriously escaped. I think that my Dad thought that Mam had released the bird on purpose as she didn't like the mess it made in the house. Infact, Mam didn't like mess of any kind and I can only describe my home environment as the nearest to sterile as one can get. She was obsessed with cleaning the house and bleaching everywhere. To the outside world she would have been the perfect Wife and Mother, a public façade that masked her and soon began to show its weaknesses bit by bit soon after. That apart, I can still feel the warmth and smell that filled the Kitchen from the Range and the constant reminders about the dangers associated with it being "hot, dangerous and burn". This very same range played a huge part in the rescue of a baby bird that I found in the garden, it had perhaps fallen out of a nearby nest or perhaps been dropped by a Predator either way it was featherless, tiny and very cold. I may have been very young but I can still visualise the little bird and with the help of my Dad I placed the tiny chick gently inside a small cardboard box which he had insulated with newspaper and straw and placed it beside the range where I attempted to feed it bread and milk or worms. Unfortunately the poor little thing didn't survive and I can't remember whether this upset me or not. I also remember lying on the settee with Mam, how I loved my Mam she was everything that I wanted her to be and it was lovely to have this 'special time' with her while my Brother was at Nursery School. We would watch the television programme "Watch with Mother" and Mam would pretend that she was interested in the programme when really she was trying to grab a sneaky mid-morning snooze. I enjoyed this time so much as it was a time when Mam wasn't busy and I could be close to her.

I can remember sitting in my pushchair with a Dutch blanket covering me when we walked Kelvin to Nursery down the enormous hill and back again. As it happens both Kelvin and I had one of these blankets, I loved mine so much that it became a favourite of mine for many years to come, in fact I was still using this blanket well into my teens, I must have a good memory as I was only 2 years old when I left the house that I was born in in Staffordshire and moved to Warwickshire. It must have been a huge decision to make but my Parents must have felt that it was the move to make. My Great Auntie Penny, Uncle Edwin and their Children plus Mam's Sister Margaret, Brother-in-Law Derek and their four Daughters moved there first and I would imagine that once they were settled they told my parents that there were good work and housing opportunities available.

While I sit here pondering I have worked out that by the time I reached 20 years old I had moved nine times, is this normal, have you moved around as much as me?

Dad used to love telling us a good story and one that he used to mock Mam about during the entire duration of their marriage was the one about the cabbage pie. It used to wind Mam up no end and as they hadn't been married long I think she felt embarrassed about the story plus she was probably just learning to cook, either way she used to get mad everytime Dad told anyone who was willing to listen how she made him a cabbage pie! How he loved this story probably more so as he never failed to get an angry reaction from Mam everytime he mentioned it which believe you and me was often. Here goes with the story, Dad's version of course ... Dad got in from his shift at the Pit and Mam proudly presented him with a pie of sorts, you see, there was an old favourite recipe in the North-East of baking a pie with just a pastry lid rather than the usual pastry surrounding the filling, the method used to hold up the pastry lid of the pie was to rest it on some upturned egg cups and then bake in the oven. Mam's pie had two flaws 1. She said that she had used up the vegetables from the Sunday dinner which was from the day before and that is how a tiny bit of cabbage came to appear in the pie; Dad says that he cut into the pie and it had cabbage in 2. Mam had used plastic egg cups to support the pie lid which obviously when the heat of the oven had reached them they melted, can you imagine the pair of them attempting to eat together during this disastrous meal with Dad laughing at Mam and Mam retaliating with the wrath of her tongue? I look forward to telling you the story of the Shepherd's Pie later on which I think is equally as funny.

I mentioned earlier that we lived close to my maternal family who had also made the move to the Midlands but maintained strong links with my extended family in the North-East. Granda Edgar was a kind, gentle, funny, easy going man who was also a Coalminer and Grandma Greta was a little petite lady who unfortunately had Rheumatoid Arthritis to contend with from quite an early age. My Granda was funny and always used to do daft things with us that made us laugh so much. He once came into the Box Room to me when I was settling down to sleep one night, we were staying at their house for the weekend you see, the next thing I heard was ghost like noises coming along the Landing and then Granda suddenly burst through the door into the room wearing a red cape (a tablecloth) and he had a fresh tomato wedged in his mouth and a raw carrot hanging out of each ear. I laughed until my stomach hurt and went to sleep as happy as a pig in muck.

I have no memories at all of my Grandma Greta being anything other than frail as she was bent forwards at the waist and crippled, which is probably why I always thought that she was short in height. This vision being shattered much later which I shall tell you about further on. My Grandma always smelt wonderful, she used Oil of Ulay cream every day and used a compact powder puff on her face and Pears Shampoo and it wasn't until I was a Teenager that I noticed that my Grandma was different from other Grandma's as she had brown hair. This was strange as everyone else that I knew at that age had grey or white hair and it wasn't until I was in my teens that I came to the conclusion that my Grandma actually had her hair dyed when she attended her weekly appointment at the little Hairdresser's Salon which was located just on the canal bridge near to the Working Men's Club. All of us (Grandchildren) knew from an early age that we couldn't sit on our Grandma's knee for a cuddle as she was in an awful lot of pain but I do remember always giving her a kiss on her cheek when I arrived and again when I left her house. Both of my Grandparents loved a bet on the Horse Racing and every day they would choose who they thought the 'Winner' was going to be and Granda would go down to the Bookies (Bookmakers) in the High Street to put their bets on, one time I remember distinctly when Grandma won £105 on an 'Accumulator' and she treated every single Grandchild to £5 each. This was a lot of money at the time and I have to say that I likened the feeling when I got my £5 to that of one similar to Charlie Bucket when he discovered one of the five 'Golden Tickets' which had been concealed inside the wrapper of a Wonka Bar, this being the story from Charlie and the Chocolate Factory.

My Grandma blamed her arthritis from being sent to London when she was very young to work "In Service" as they called it as a Servant in one of the "Big Houses". She said that all the floor scrubbing did nothing to help her with the pain and inflammation in her knees and other joints. It must have been a really frightening experience travelling all the way to London alone at such a young age particularly as Grandma had to leave her home and family behind. Anyway my Grandma felt that the damp in the house that they eventually moved into was due to the fact that a Billboard which was used for advertising and was fixed to the gable end of the property was the culprit of the damp situation as she reckoned that the damp was getting trapped inside the house which then led to it getting into her joints.

Granda had Angina which is a pain that occurs in the chest when the blood supply to the muscles of the heart is restricted; the arteries supplying the heart become hardened and narrowed and the pain and discomfort supposedly feels like a dull, heavy or tight pain in the chest that can sometimes spread to the left arm, neck, jaw or back and many a time I have seen him sitting with a tablet under his tongue trying to ease the discomfort. He also had Coal Workers' Pneumoconiosis (CWP) which is caused by the inhalation and retention of coal dust in the lungs; I have been led to believe that this tends to have a time lap of about 10 years before it presents any physical signs.

My Granda used to sit very patiently on the Wing backed chair which was next to the fire in the Living room while I used to brush his hair with a little blue soft baby brush. He had an enormous amount of patience with everyone, infact I have never seen or heard him lose his temper or become vexed with any of us and I always used to love it when he used to give us what he called a 'big sloppy kiss'. This was always on our arrival and also when leaving the house and I used to laugh as it was kind of similar to having a big sloppy lick from a Boxer dog.

My Grandparents stayed in the village when we moved to Warwickshire and we used to visit them regularly particularly a Friday night until a Sunday. We loved these weekends as the family would get together at the local Working Men's Club and

Kelvin and I stayed in on the Friday night but were allowed to go to the Club on the Saturday night where we would watch the family play Bingo, watch a *Turn and generally have a good catch up with each other. We always sat in the same seats on the same table in the Big Room of the Club which I think everyone referred to as 'The Concert Room' and it seemed that most families did this too with a lot of families choosing to take a mini picnic type supper with them which would include sandwiches, pork pie, sausage rolls and hard boiled eggs which I thought was strange particularly when they got their salt cellar out of their handbags ready for the eggs. We never took anything to eat with us preferring instead to choose our Supper from the blue, scruffy looking Mobile Fish and Chip van which was parked outside The Club.

It served a rather unusual choice of mushy peas as they had so much food colouring added to them that they looked luminous. Instead we would wait until we got back to Grandma and Granda's for Ham and Pease Puddin sandwiches, this savoury pudding is made from split peas flavoured with ham and eaten hot or cold, originally this being an industrial North Eastern delicacy that was traditionally served with Stottie Cakes, I hate Pease Puddin but the hand carved ham that my Grandparents boiled was always delicious.

"Pease pudding hot, Pease pudding cold, Pease pudding in the pot, nine days old".

As I sit writing, the memories come flooding back of my Grandparents house in Gainsborough Road, the Kitchen with the Belfast Sink which I can recall having a bath in when I was a Toddler, the tall Pantry stocked to the brim with all sorts of provisions to the point where you would have thought there was a War on as they were keeping stock levels high, the open coal fire, round table and four chairs and last but not least the huge cupboard under the stairs that housed everything from

---

* Turn – Geordie name for 'Live' entertainment.

stepladders, lawnmower, gardening tools to spare caps, coats, boots and even the twin tub washing machine. In the Kitchen Granda also had a very special drawer which he had all manner of 'odds and sods' in such as screwdrivers, pliers, sticky tape, bouncy balls, the famous blue baby brush, right down to numerous sizes of jubilee clips, screws and nuts and bolts. If the contents of that drawer couldn't fix your DIY problem then nothing could believe me as my Granda was an absolute whizz repairing most things.

When I was visiting I used to get up early in a morning to find my Granda sitting in the Kitchen in front of the coal fire which he had just lit; no matter what time of the year it was he always used to be wearing his slippers, trousers and white cotton vest and would be smoking one of his Woodbine *Tabs. Grandma preferred him to limit himself to a pack of ten tabs per day but I have no doubt that he was sneakily topping his ten pack up from a secret stash. I never recalled him ever smoking a full tab always preferring to nip it out part way and because Woodbines never had a filter in them he used to smoke them right the way down almost to his index finger and thumb and I felt for sure that he would burn himself. He would say "You just sit there Hinny and get warm while I make you some funny jam on toast and a cup of strong tea", I think the referral to the tea was from when he was a *Bairn and the teapot would always be on the fire keeping warm with a spoonful of tea leaves being added to the pot randomly throughout the day. The result would be a very strong black brew being offered to all. A brew of tea would always be made with the upmost of care in our family using a large metal teapot along with the preferred choice of loose tealeaves which would make a very strong brew and the funny jam I later discovered was infact Robertson's Marmalade and Granda used to save the Robertson's Golly tokens which were on the labels attached to the side of the jars. When he had collected enough tokens

---

* Tabs - Geordie name for Cigarettes.

* Bairn - Geordie name for Child.

he would send off for a new Golly Badge, there were loads to collect and funnily enough I carried on the tradition with my Son when he was born, he has 25 in total but sadly he should have had much more. Back in those days they were known as 'Golliwogs' but this isn't politically correct to say now and so they have since been renamed 'Golly' badges.

Once the fire was well established my Granda would take my Grandma a cup of tea and a slice of jam on bread up to her which she ate whilst sitting on the edge of their big double bed. She used to have to take her time getting up and as such had to do things bit by bit so that she could ease her stiff joints into moving more freely. This was a painful process for my Grandma and was awful to see her in so much pain. After breakfast Granda would then help to wash and dress Grandma before returning downstairs where he would get on with the chores for the day which included shopping, cleaning, preparing their meals and anything else that cropped up during the day.

My Brother and I had fun in the cupboard under the stairs. We used to play 'Cops and Robbers' or 'Detectives' and had a full wardrobe to choose from which enabled us to look the part. There was such a distinctive smell in the cupboard, not an unpleasant one but one that I will never forget and funnily enough when my Grandparents later moved the very same smell was in their new storage cupboard.

My Grandparents house had an L shaped Living Room which had had the coal fire removed and replaced with a gas fire. This soon became the stage area for my Brother as he used to stand with his back to the fire playing an imaginary guitar pretending to be Gary Glitter and singing "I'm the Leader of the Gang (I am!)" this was a top hit for British Rock Singer Gary and it reached number 1 of the UK Top 40 in July 1973. Also in this room there were two huge windows which were at opposite ends to each other, net curtains hung at the windows to aid privacy. It seemed that Mam also had a love of net curtains as every place we lived in she had nets hanging at all the windows, needless to say that I hate nets because they remind me of my Mam. Grandma's pride and joy was also in this room, her china display cabinet which housed her prized possession "a Crinoline Lady teapot" which I think my Uncle Edgar had bought for her, some 'nice' drinking glasses, their Silver Wedding Anniversary gifts and last but by no means least a bottle of Martell Brandy (for Medicinal purposes only, mainly shock) and a bottle of Warnink's Advocat (for Christmas). God forbid anyone who dared to go near that cabinet and God help you if you left your finger marks upon the glass as Holy Hell would prevail. Leading from the Living room into the Hallway you would think that you had stepped into "The Lion, The Witch and The Wardrobe" as it was like going into another world, more like the North Pole to be fair as I have never felt *cald like it. Up the stairs which were slightly curved was the separate toilet which was very dark indeed as it had the tiniest window which was always left slightly ajar, the pink bathroom was next which accommodated the airing cupboard and then a double bedroom which overlooked the back garden on one side, on the opposite side of the house and facing the front of the property was my Grandparent's huge bedroom and finally the last room in the house the Box room. All the bedrooms had Lino on the floor and a rug centralised on top of the lino which the bed was positioned on top of. My Brother and I had fun playing hide and seek along with other games upstairs. We must have been feeling charitable to each other to even consider giving each other the time of day either that or we were just incredibly bored.

The back garden had a concrete coal bunker and a lawn area which was positioned on a slight incline. A gate led out to the Council Garages which were directly behind the property which was really handy for my Granda as he rented one of the garages for his car which over the years he had many of: Morris Oxford, Austin Cambridge, Vauxhall Victor and Hillman

---

* Cald - Geordie word for cold.

Hunter to name but a few. The front garden was quite large with a flat lawn and was completely bordered by flowerbeds including the dreaded Roses. My Granda used to keep the gardens neat and tidy with the aid of his sky blue Qualcast Concorde Lawnmower and I used to spend hours in the front garden mainly swinging around and around on the two metal poles that provided support to the canopy that sheltered the front door. The front garden was also the scene of a crash one day when a lorry came hurtling out of control down the road and veered off across the grass verge and pavement and smashed straight into the dividing garden wall which separated the front garden from their Neighbours.

As we talk about my birthplace I wonder if you can name anyone famous who was born there. Now then I would like to test your memory and ask if you can remember the Stage Actor Brewster Mason, he was born there exactly 22 years to the day before my Dad was born in 1922; he was a notable character of the Royal Shakespeare Company between 1963-1987 and also made appearances in many television plays and series including: The Affair 1962, The Palliser's 1974, Quatermass 1979 and Tales of the unexpected 1980-81. Brewster's film appearances include The Dambusters 1954 and Private Potter 1962 and tragically he died after a fall while playing the title role in Richard II, I guess the only comfort here was that he died doing what he loved. Mark Abraham Bright former Footballer and now Sports pundit was born in 1962 and attended the local High School which was also the school that my Son attended and is situated on the same road that my Grandparents lived. Maybe you have already made the link between my birthplace and the Black Panther, otherwise known as Donald Nappey? He later changed his name to Neilson after his Daughter was born so that she did not have to endure years of bullying about her last name; Donald had had a hard time during his school years and he didn't want his Daughter to go through the same thing. He was an Armed Robber who murdered three people during eighteen robberies of Sub-Post Offices from 1971-1974, his fourth and last victim was in 1975 of seventeen year old

Heiress from Highley in Shropshire called Lesley Whittle. The Whittle case made him Britain's most wanted man during the mid-70's and he was sentenced to Life Imprisonment in 1976 after Lesley's body was discovered hanging from a wire at the bottom of the drainage shaft from where he had tethered her at a local Pool. After Neilson's capture he was interviewed at the local Police Station where he confessed to kidnapping Lesley. His life and crimes were portrayed in the 1977 film The Black Panther which was directed by Ian Merrick and starred Donald Sumpter as Neilson, as it happens we moved back to my birthplace shortly after the Black Panther was caught and lived in a Ground Floor Flat where my bedroom backed onto the Woods of the Pool and Park area. I was not keen on my location as I felt frightened for a number of reasons 1. My bedroom window faced the woods and without any external lighting it became a scary place after dark and 2. I used to walk past the shaft where Lesley Whittle had died on my way to my Auntie May's and Uncle Joe's. The shaft has a thick metal bar padlocked across it and strangely enough when I was out playing with my friends I found a garden spade lying on top of it, to this day have no idea why it was there but needless to say it spooked me.

Chapter 4

Evil Woman – (Electric Light Orchestra)

Now moving around the Country a lot can cause some issues particularly with simple everyday tasks for example I used to get really confused about buying Bread Rolls depending on my location and if I bought Bread in Warwickshire I used to ask for Batches, when I tried to ask for Batches in Staffordshire they hadn't a clue what I was asking for until I pointed to the soft white rolls in the shop window where I was met with the curt reply "They are called Baps young lady", blinking heck "Sorry"! Finally to the North-East to buy Stottie Bread or Cakes as they are sometimes called which was a far easier transaction and I have to say a far more pleasant one as the Shop Assistant would always have a bit of a chat with me. Do you think that it is strange how on depending on location people meet and greet you in such varying ways? I recall visiting the local Newsagent with my Dad in the Village that he was born in and as soon as we walked into the shop the Shopkeeper greeted my Dad with "Alreet Geordie" to which my Dad responded "Alreet Paki"!!!

I then explained to my Dad that we were not allowed to say Paki and instead would have said that they were a Pakistani so that we did not cause any offence. Dad responded by saying that it wasn't like that up there and it was just the same when he walked into the local 'Chinkys', by now my Son who was about 6 years old at the time was falling about laughing when he asked his Grandad if we were going to the 'Chinkys' and my response was to swiftly correct him by saying that it was actually the Chinese Take-away and that it was very important that he always referred to Chinese people by the correct term if he wanted to avoid upsetting someone. I know for a fact that in the North-East everyone says Hello to each other in the Street regardless of whether or not they know each other which is definitely not the case elsewhere in the Country.

The two main Occupations in North Staffordshire were the Pits and the Pots (Potteries) which meant that people of these specific classes spent most of their days in close proximity with people with the same way of speaking. Dialects are therefore diluted when there is a mobility of the population and are strengthened when there is a concentration of people. People in North Staffordshire tend to call everyone "Duck". This has nothing to do with the Bird by the way and is said to come from the Saxon word 'ducas' which was meant as a term of respect similar to the middle English 'duc', 'duk' which means Leader or Commander from which the title 'Duke' and the old French word 'Duchee' comes from. It was from these origins that 'Duck' became firstly a greeting and then a term of endearment.

Right where was I? Let's get back to the story … they say that time stops for no man and by the time that my Brother was 4 and I was 2, we moved to a small Pit Village which is situated near to Coventry City Centre in Warwickshire. We lived over a period of time in two houses, one being on a steep hill which I mentioned earlier and the other being the last house in a cul-de-sac. This house was what they called a Cornish Style house which had Prefabricated Reinforced Concrete (PRC) exterior walls. It was quite an odd looking house but must have been a very popular one as 30,000 were built at the time. The house came with a huge corner plot garden which was surrounded by six foot chain link fencing and a driveway leading to a detached asbestos garage overlooking fields for miles and miles. At first I liked my new house as I can remember feeling happy and safe there, little did I know that just a few years later I would refer to the house as the 'House of Horror'. It had a small Kitchen which we referred to as the Scullery and the back door led out to the coal bunker and the back garden, this small room had the bonus of a medium sized window which was on the gable end of the property and overlooked the garage, inside was a sink and drainer, gas cooker with overhead grill, fridge freezer and twin tub washing machine. Leading from the Scullery was the Breakfast Room which had an open coal fire and built in floor to ceiling wooden cupboards either side of the fireplace, a teak sideboard, fold away dining table with four matching chairs and a bed sofa, all the appliances and furniture were modern and it is fair to say that we wanted for nothing. The Breakfast Room had a large window which comprised of three smaller windows which were joined together and gave the impression of one huge sized window that almost completely filled one of the walls. Leading into the Hallway and immediately to the right was a built in cupboard underneath the staircase where we stored our coats, then the Living room to the left which had similar style windows to the Breakfast Room but also contained a modern gas fire and fireplace, a brown and gold three piece suite, shiny gold striped floor length curtains, television and a very modern radiogram of which three Capodimonte Ornaments sat proudly upon, and last but not least the very expensive autumn coloured Axminster carpet that cost the grand sum of £17 per square yard, something that not many people could afford to pay in those days.

It was over a period of time that the Television and Radiogram became Mam's tools to wind my Dad up when he was trying to sleep after a night shift. It was usually following an argument and because their bedroom was at the back of the house overlooking the garden and fields and the Living Room was at the front of the house that it became a War Zone, logistically there was quite a distance between the two rooms in question but still the noise was so loud from both pieces of electrical equipment that it still managed to travel thus making it harder for Dad to sleep. Mam used to put the Television or Radiogram on full blast when Dad was just settling off to sleep and he used to calmly come downstairs and walk into the Living Room and turn down the volume. He would no sooner get back into bed and be dozing off again when Mam used to turn the volume up again and so Dad would repeat his trip down and back up again over and over. I think he must have been fuming inside but not wanting to alarm or frighten us he calmly kept his anger under control and sometime later I remember witnessing this 'upping and downing' and Dad came into the room and threatened to put his foot through the television but still Mam did not relent. However, his next visit was the winner of the argument; he calmly cut the plug off the television with a pair of scissors and for once in her life Mam was left speechless!

The front door had three horizontal panes of obscure glass above the letterbox which was central in the door, from the front door the stairs led up to the first floor where a separate toilet with an overhead cistern and pull chain were fixed high up to the wall and a slim line window where when you were seated on the toilet the window was positioned behind your back, the bathroom was next to the toilet and again had a slim line window infront of the wash hand basin and a full size bath tub. Mam and Dad's bedroom contained a lovely set of Teak bedroom furniture which was made up of a dressing table, double wardrobe, single wardrobe and double bed. My room which was the largest of the three bedrooms and contained a double bed, a floor to ceiling built in storage cupboard, shiny effect chest of drawers that had a secret hinged lid that also provided a platform for two cuddly Koala's and a Spanish style Dancer wearing a traditional Flamenco dress to sit proudly upon. I have no idea where the Koala's or Dancer came from but assume they were given as gifts. I used to be turfed out of my turquoise blue, white and purple decorated bedroom on a regular basis so that we could accommodate our many Visitors to the house which sadly meant one thing and that was that I had to sleep on the bottom bunk bed in my Brother's room which was just next door to mine. His room was a Box room aptly named as it sat above the staircase and contained a set of bunk beds which were constructed of a tubular metal frame and were similar in colour to copper piping. It was never a good idea for Kelvin and I to share as we used to fight one another like 'Cat and Dog'. My Brother's room also contained a purpose built wooden box or platform which Mam used as the place to neatly store books, anything from my Dad's Readers Digests to Paperbacks and I can clearly recall that I was terrified of one particular book that always appeared to be on clear view at the end of the shelf that had a human skull illustrated on the front cover and one real eye ball that appeared to follow me around the room. No matter how many times I tried to conceal this book in amongst the others it would miraculously appear at the end of the shelf again. Hmm, was this down to my Brother or my Mam? Also in the corner of Kelvin's room was a large, strong cardboard box which contained all of our Toys and Games. The top of the box was covered with a crisp, white linen tablecloth which was draped over the top and sides in order to try and hide the contents and although me and my Brother both longed to get into it to have a good rummage we were always discouraged from getting anything out of the box for fear of making a mess.

There were two rules that Kelvin and I had to obey with regards to the toilet, 1. Under no circumstances must we bolt the door shut in case we got locked in and 2. Always shout down for assistance when we had completed our business, I can still hear myself calling "Finished! Come and wipe me bum"! One night when I was having a tiddle on the loo there was a power cut, Holy Hell let loose as I screamed to find my slipper in the dark whilst still sitting on the actual toilet itself? The way I carried on you would have thought that murder had been committed. I still to this day do not understand why I was making such a fuss as it's not even like we were Kids that had to have a night light on when we were in bed. Oh no, there was none of that Mamby Pamby business going on with us, in fact just the opposite as Mam insisted that when we were babies we didn't become noise sensitive and as such it was nothing for Mam to be ramming the hoover under my pram while I was sleeping, something which I must admit I did with my Son and he can sleep through anything to the point where I feel fairly confident that he could sleep on a washing line if he had to.

The bed sofa which was in the Breakfast Room was invaluable especially as our family had always travelled a fair way from either Staffordshire or the North-East, it also became my Island of Safety when Mam was hoovering as I was terrified of it thinking that it was going to suck me up if I got in its way and as such Mam always thought it was funny to chase me with it. I used to throw myself upon the sofa and tuck my knees right up under my chin and hug myself for protection. This was not my only fear as it is only fair to let you know at this point that I have an issue with being lost and I fear that it stems from my childhood and was triggered following something that happened to me soon after we moved to the house in the cul-de-sac. Mam had taken me into the City Centre one Saturday morning to do some shopping, I was only small, wearing some T bar shoes, tights and a little dress and a thick woollen coat that Mam had knit for me, Mam was always knitting things for me and my Brother and we both developed a phobia against her creations as firstly our garments were always matching and secondly if it was a jumper we always used to dread taking the jumper off as she had the habit of knitting the neck and cuffs so tight supposedly to maintain the jumpers shape that when the dreaded "Hands up for Jesus" was said both Kelvin and I used to cringe and cry out in pain as she pulled the jumpers up and over our faces causing great pain coupled with a burning sensation on our ears and nose as she wrenched the jumper off over our heads. Anyway back to being lost ... at some point I became aware that something wasn't quite right and can remember looking around for Mam but she wasn't there, she had disappeared into thin air and as a result I was lost! I stayed exactly where I was and turned around and around on the spot not daring to move an inch either way for fear of getting into further trouble. My eyes were frantically darting in every direction until tears began to well up, my anxiety heightened to the point where I ended up bawling my eyes out until a Stranger came to my rescue. It was no good I had to face facts and the fact was that I was lost in a ginormous concrete jungle. I was distraught, the Stranger was trying their best to console me but I was having none of it and then all of a sudden Mam appeared from behind the concrete pillar laughing at me, she had been there all the time watching me panic and I hadn't really been lost at all. Afterwards she took me into our favourite Fish & Chip Restaurant which was located next to the Bus Station just past the Motor Museum, once inside I proceeded to wet myself, all down my lovely tights and into my shoes, brilliant! The perfect ending to a perfect day NOT! I am sure it is from this incident that I have terrible anxiety about travelling to places and becoming lost, I just panic in unfamiliar surroundings and I'm not much better travelling to and from routes that I have done repeatedly time and time again, for example, when travelling to the North-East I have the Sat Nav programmed, a bullet pointed list of hand written directions blue tacked to the front of the glove box and my Dad calling me at least three times en route so that he could track my whereabouts. My Dad on the other hand never had any problems navigating his way around the country as he had a simple solution ... Incorporate "nice toilets" as part of your route and you will never go wrong! I have to be honest here though as I have never managed to locate the "nice toilets" that he always used to rave about in Kirkby Stephens, funny how he always referred to them as nice as I'm sure he has been in some really rough ones during his travels.

It was while we were living in the cul-de-sac that we got a dog called Charlie who was named after my Granda Edgar's dog Charlie who as it happens is buried in the back garden of my Grandparents house. We were over the moon with our beautiful German shepherd puppy but our joy was short-lived as we didn't know it at the time but his days were numbered with our Mam, you see she had had the Breakfast Room refurbished with new decoration, furniture and carpet and within only a week of Charlie coming to live with us he proceeded to demolish the place including chewing sixteen chair legs plus the four table legs, the sideboard legs and just to finish the job off properly he tore the new carpet up. God, I was smug to see Mam's distress and wanted to praise Charlie to high heaven as I thought he had got one up on Mam but my glee was short lived when I returned home from school later the following day to discover he had gone and that was that. There was quite clearly no discussion about her decision as it was clear she was not going to budge on bringing him home. Just a few weeks later Mam told us she was going to show us a surprise and drove us to the place which happened to be where Charlie had been rehomed. It was pitiful to see him; he was chained to a kennel in a Scrap Yard and was filthy. It broke my heart to see him like that and now when I think back to that day she must have had a cruel heart to show her children their Puppy living like that especially as he immediately recognised us. I don't think any of us ever forgave her for that especially my Dad and in later years he was able to rescue a beautiful German shepherd who he called Zak who he adored from day one. They had twelve wonderful years together and their daily routine was to walk around the Lakes and surrounding areas of the village twice a day, Zak in return for this wonderful life of freedom was my Dad's Loyal Companion and it was clear to see from both of them how much they adored one another, they were perfect together. Ironically Zak passed away peacefully the week before Dad went into hospital to have Colon Surgery. The date was the 17th November 2008, a date that I shall not forget even though I wish I could as the date was the beginning of the end for my Dad. As I think about Zak passing away it was just like he could sense my Dad's anxiety about leaving him for the rest of the family to look after until he was out of Hospital and back on his feet again and he died peacefully in his sleep in the place he loved so much. His death was a big loss for my Dad and his walks were obviously never the same again. My Dad had done a fine job of training Zak and once they were over the Lakes he would let him off the lead for a run and when he saw another dog approaching them Zak would return to Dad and pop his own head through into his collar and lead again. What a clever dog! Funny thing is though that Zak would not settle in my Dads bungalow and so he lived over in the Stables which were just a few footsteps across the Lane to the back of Dads place. He was a brilliant Guard dog and protected the retired Race Horses, Pigeons and Ducks etc. that my Dad used to acquire in some shape or form. Thinking about it he was such a funny dog really as he had a routine the same as my Dads and he would be waiting for my Dad bang on 5pm which is the time when Dad used to feed him, this was also the case at 8am and 4pm every day as that was the time when they went for their walks. I wonder if a dog could be Autistic because he used to be waiting for my Dad just like he had timed his appearance.

The teak sideboard was part of another Crime Scene not long after Charlie had gone. Mam had noticed that one of her Lipsticks and pink Nail Varnishes had mysteriously disappeared from her Dressing Table only to discover that they had been used as a part of some very abstract art work in the Breakfast Room where much to her horror her beautiful sideboard had been decorated with the missing cosmetics and to make matters worse my Brother blamed me, it's a really good job that he didn't get away with that one and that she knew who the real Culprit was, to this day I don't know what actually gave the game away but I am thankful that I didn't receive a belting for it.

There was no boundary to Mam's cruelty and Dad was devastated when after another almighty row she picked up his Silver Pocket Watch which had been left to him by his Da just before he had passed away and she purposely dropped it on the floor and stamped on it with her foot smashing it into pieces. My Dad was heartbroken as the watch meant so much to him and was irreplaceable. He retaliated back by picking the pieces of the watch up and throwing it at her narrowly missing her head.

Many, many years later on my Wedding Day my new Husband and I presented Dad with a Gold Pocket Watch which I hoped would go some way to healing his broken heart. I don't think it did but he treasured it all the same and passed it on to his Grandson on his 21st birthday, who treasures it equally along with some of his Grandad's cigarette lighters from way back in the days when he smoked his Cowboy Cigarettes. Dad would make these tabs himself with the loose Tobacco rolled in brown liquorice papers and he used to wind my Son up by saying that he should consider himself lucky to have a Grandad that looked the double of Clint Eastwood, my Boy just used to shrug his shoulders and laugh to the point where he wasn't at all surprised as to what his Grandad was going to say next.

Also while we were living in this house we had a white Ford Cortina Estate car and Mam had a Moped which I think she acquired from my Auntie Penny. She had a white open faced crash helmet which I loved to wear when I was riding my bike pretending it was a motorbike. I even went as far as to try and imitate the sounds of the engine, thinking back to those days brings a smile to my face especially as I bet I looked and sounded like a right numpty bombing around the pavements on my little bike making ridiculous noises. A few years later we replaced the old white car with a real bobby dazzler of one which was a metallic blue Toyota Crown Saloon. We felt like Royalty in it as the inside was really plush to the point where it not only had an ashtray fitted in the front of the vehicle but it had one in the back too. It had loads and loads of gadgets, two that stood out to me were the electric windows and an aerial that I was mesmerised with as it automatically went up and down dependant on whether or not we were switching the radio on or off, this car had an Automatic Transmission which I swear I can still hear the hum of the engine to this day. Mam thought she was "It" driving around the village; she was a proper "Show Off" and would purposely pull over and offer people a lift just so she could show the car off even when we weren't even going in their direction. For those of you who are not familiar with Toyota Crowns they are a premium medium to full-size Luxury Sedan that Toyota primarily aimed at the Japanese market but they also have a much sinister purpose as they are used in Iraq as the choice of wheels chosen by Gangs, this is because they offer the ideal blend of speed and affordability for an Assassin/Kidnapper about town and very often you will hear "Beware or you'll end up in a Toyota Crown" as so many of these cars have been used in Hits, Car Bombs and Abductions so much so that the Army and Police tend to automatically search them at Checkpoints.

The old white car is quite distinctive in my memory as I spent numerous times travelling lying stretched out asleep on the back seat of the car with Kelvin and Dad upfront driving through the Moors late into the night and early morning, this was a time before the wearing of seatbelts was made compulsory and travelling from Warwickshire to the North-East was a lengthy process and also the time when I became aware of Mam and Dad's issues with one another. You see my Parents argued and fought with each other to the point where Mam would physically attack Dad with whatever she could get her hands on, one time she walloped him on the funny bone of his elbow with the big red ball end of the fire poker that was on the hearth of the fireplace in the Breakfast Room, an injury that Dad said he could still feel to this day if he caught his elbow awkwardly. My Dad found it hard to cope with his feelings and thoughts and seemed to think it was a sign of weakness on his part that Mam had got the better of him by driving him to lose his temper with her. He wasn't making excuses because whatever a person does to you it does not give you the right to physically attack them regardless of what they may have done but Mam somewhere along the line had gained the ability to wind him up so much that sometimes he slapped her across her face. He hated himself for this but still it happened and on more than one occasion, sometimes I believe fists were used too and with him being such a gentle, quiet chap I don't think he ever forgave himself for losing control, something that he has never done before or after his marriage to my Mam. Following these incidents Dad would calmly pack a suitcase and put me and Kelvin in the car and off we would go to the North-East. My Brother said that we used to doze on the journey, me more so than him and he remembers one journey in particular where we both happened to be wearing our matching tracksuits, his being navy blue and white and mine red and white and apart from that Dad drove the journey more or less in silence with the monotony only being broken by Dad chain smoking his Embassy Regal tabs, sometimes the odd stop at a Roadside Cafe or Truck Driver Stop would also ease the monotony and where we would have a cup of tea and maybe something to eat.

Anyway back to our destination, to my Dad's Sister's place Auntie Marjorie's and Uncle Timothy's and to a place of peace and calm. I will never forget the three of us standing on their doorstep knocking at 6am much to their surprise. They were wonderful and soon got us settled down as we were quite bewildered as to what was going on particularly in the early days. Dad would produce a couple of suitcases with our clothes bundled into and my Auntie Marjorie would set about sorting our beds etc. she would then sit in front of the open coal fire in the Living Room and get the long toasting fork out to make some fireside toast for us or bake us our favourite corned beef, potato and onion pie or cakes and just totally indulge us. My Auntie Marjorie and Uncle Timothy were never able to have children but they were just the best people to be around as they were so affectionate and we felt safe with them. It's funny but since I started to write this book I had a chat with my Auntie Marjorie and she said that years ago people didn't talk about Infertility unlike today; she said it is more like saying "God Bless You".

On one of these trips to we even travelled one Christmas night, we had only opened our presents in the morning and here we were travelling to the North-East with the most difficult of choices to make ... Dad said to choose just three toys each to take with us, this was hard but in the end I settled on my Disney Peel and Glitter Art Set and I can't remember what the other two were for me and I certainly can't remember what Kelvin took? Funny thing is that I am even more surprised that Mam even bought me the Glitter Set as can you imagine how much mess it could have made?

While we were staying over at our Auntie and Uncle's house there would always be the inevitable knock at the front door, both me and Kelvin would go upstairs very quietly with our Dad where we would hear the *Polis asking my Auntie Marjorie if my Dad was there and my Auntie would always say "No", this little white lie used to buy us about a week of grace away from our Mam. Dad once told me that when I was 2 and Kelvin 4 a Psychiatrist asked him to sign a consent form agreeing to have our Mam Sectioned in a Mental Hospital. Dad said it was his biggest regret of his life not doing so but he felt that he didn't have a choice as he was hundreds of miles away from any family support in a house that was tied to his job and a job that was shift work. How could he manage to look after a 2 and 4 year old and work etc. It is only now as a Parent that I can begin to understand the turmoil he must have gone through trying to do his best for all of us, as it was it was always the case that we had to return to Mam and our Parents would try and "patch things up", when this happened we would kind of go into what I would now call the Honeymoon period again.

It was an odd situation really as when we first got home from one of these trips and saw Mam for the first time she would be sporting a black eye or broken nose and it wasn't a very nice thing to see especially if you didn't quite know what was going on plus I was never sure whether Dad had done this to Mam before we left or if Mam had sustained the bruises from someone else while we had been away. Mam also had this habit of appearing to be quite subdued and this used to

---

* Polis – Geordie word for Police.

leave me feeling quite sorry for her which then left me with the strangest feeling because I felt guilty feeling the way I did about my Mam because I knew that I loved her but I didn't like the way she behaved at times and because of this she used to make me feel quite anxious and sometimes frightened as I didn't know what was going to happen next after all it wasn't like I could run to the Pit and fetch my Dad out of work was it? After all he was more or less cut off from the world outside working underground so at times I felt quite helpless. Infact, it wasn't until I travelled to Poland many years later and visited The Wieliczka Salt Mine could I relate more accurately to my Dad's working conditions as I can honestly say that the descent down into the Mine felt like I was travelling deep down to Hell, it did nothing to soothe my thoughts when the Polish Guide kept referring to "The Chambre" (Chamber) wherever we stopped to see the next attraction. The Salt Mine is located in the town of Wieliczka in Southern Poland and lies within the Krakow Metropolitan area. It reaches a depth of 1073ft and is over 178 miles long and was built in the 13th Century, produced Table Salt continuously until 2007. In the early centuries of our Country's history I know that Coal was not really called for as our Forests were extensive and therefore abundant meaning that there was little call for Coal. However, Coal was used to a considerable extent in the manufacture of Salt from the seashore usually associated with Salt-pans. Salt making required a regular supply of Coal and this is how the two industries of Salt making and Coal mining grew up side by side.

Now my mind is racing with my thoughts … I suppose I just thought that I had to love my Mam regardless of what she did, then I used to feel guilty mainly because I had questioned our bond as I knew from quite an early age that not only did I love my Dad but I liked him a lot too. Fortunately through all of this I had the ability to reason that my Parents were completely different people, after all they were supposed to be weren't they? They both had good and bad points it was just hard for me trying to balance the bad points with my Mam and this would make me feel very confused and in turmoil as I am sure that I shouldn't have been feeling anything other than happy-go-lucky at this age. I suppose if I could sum it up I felt it was my duty to love her even though it would have been sad not to live with both of my Parents I felt settled and safe with Dad and didn't really want to be with my Mam without my Dad being there to oversee things. This unsettling feeling never left me and only got worse as the years rolled on, which is a shame really as I now know that I shouldn't have had the weight of those thoughts on my mind or the feeling of being responsible for my Mam and I have searched through the back of my mind over and over again to look for an answer to what triggered my thoughts and I think it was when I started to compare my Mam's behaviour with that of my friends Mums and quickly concluding that no matter which way I tried to dress it up my Mam was different from any of my friends Mums. Their Mum's didn't behave like mine no matter how much I wished that they did. I wished above all else that my Mam was different but sadly this was not to be and had I known then what I know now I could have saved myself a whole load of heartache, infact I know it sounds really harsh but I used to wish that I had never been born.

Chapter 5

Seasons in the Sun – (Terry Jacks)

Dad loved walking and a day wouldn't go by where he didn't have a walk but the difference was that when my Parents were on the "patch it up honeymoon period" Mam would make an effort and join us on our walks too. A favourite walk of ours was when we used to go and feed the Ducks and then call at the Farm on the way home to buy some Duck eggs. Dad and I loved Duck eggs particularly as they had the most enormous yolks that easily accommodated my toasted soldiers. On one of these walks Mam wore a blue dress and did Handstands and Cartwheels on the Playing Field next to our house, we also had a game of Rounder's with the other kids and when we got "knocked out" we sat on the embankment in the sunshine watching the rest of our teams play. I used to think how lucky I was to have such young and fun parents when most of my friends had parents that were a lot older than mine, sadly this special time with my Parents didn't last.

The Playing Field was an excellent play area although it did have a downside to it ... it had the Grumpy Old Caretaker's house which was situated at the very top of the field in-between the field and the Playground, two Tennis Courts and a Pavilion of which accommodated the Council Play Scheme and the Tufty Club (a spin off from the Royal Society for the Prevention Accidents, RoSPA) of which I was proudly a Member of both. The Tufty Club was founded in 1953 by the late Elsie Mills MBE and the original stories featured a Squirrel and his friends with the intention of introducing clear and simple safety messages for children. Tufty was accompanied by Minnie Mole and the naughty Willy Weasel along with Mrs Owl the Teacher and Policeman Badger. Behind the Pavilion was the Park which had a slide, swings, monkey bars, roundabout, see-saw and climbing frame and I spent hours playing there along with the other kids. Just off from the Park were two Gulley's that all the Kids used as a cut through to all three of the schools, the Gulley's were bordered on one side by an assortment of either wooden or chain-link fencing. On the opposite side to the Gulley's was a narrow Brook and trees, beyond this the area opened up into farm land mainly for grazing cattle. As it happened the Farm beyond had a fantastic supply of food scraps from our School Kitchens which was fed to the Pigs in the form of Pig Swill, which for those of you who don't know Pig Swill is food mixed with water, something that we are no longer allowed to do due to the increasing risk of Foot and Mouth disease. The Gulley's were enchanting as they had Wild Flowers growing all over even in the most random locations, the smells were amazing from the habitat and I loved to hear the Birds singing as I skipped along to and from School, the Rabbits showed no fear either as they were quite used to seeing Humans, there wasn't anything that spoiled this area, no Tarmac Path just hard baked earth where natural puddles could form, I can't even remember seeing any litter but I'm sure that my memory must be flawed here as there must have been some litter surely.

On the boundary of the Park was the only pub in the village called The Raven which was built in 1964 and had an 'Outdoor' hatch which was similar to an Off Licence, from here Snacks could be purchased along with Alcohol and Soft drinks. Those of you of a certain age will remember fondly the profitable pastime of taking empty 'Pop' bottles back to the shop to collect cash refunds, this supplemented Kid's Pocket Money and helped to keep litter down and encouraged green habits long before Recycling became a buzzword. Now David Cameron is considering bringing back deposit refunds as environmental concerns take on a new urgency. The pub had an L shaped car park and an enormous Beer Garden to the rear of the property which was enclosed by a six foot slatted wooden fence. We could see into the Beer Garden from the top of either the slide or the monkey frame and on reflection I think the Pub covered a significant area of land, more than most Public Houses did anyway. We used to spend some of our time in the "Games Room" which had a Dart Board, Pool Table and Card Tables and also had wooden type benches in there and after Dad left we would very often track Mam down in there and if she was in a good mood she would treat us to a small bottle of fizzy pop and a packet of crisps, if not, we had to clear off and play, either way she kept us waiting for quite a long time before she was ready to come home.

Further along the road was the Co-op, the Co-op Butchers and a Fish and Chip shop and just a short walk away would find you in the Village where a set of shops which we used to call the Precinct would be, these included the Post Office of which, once Dad had left, Mam emptied mine and Kelvins Savings Accounts, a Chemist's, Toy shop, Wool shop, VG Mini Market and Hardware Store along with other General Stores, it was a lovely little shopping area.

I can remember Mam pushing me around the VG shop in my pushchair and at the time my Auntie Penny was working there and it was always lovely to see her as she was so nice to me and she had the best smile in the world which would put anyone at ease. The shops were made up of two rows facing one another which had steps leading down the centre and raised flower beds dotted in-between which always looked nice and were built from brick. Just a few strides away was the nearest Public Telephone Box which became a place that I frequented in the early hours of the morning almost on a daily basis once Dad had left. If I close my eyes now I can recapture the smell or should I say stench from the urine inside there, God only knows why people had to wee in there, the bright red paint on the Georgian style metal work and the concrete base and how cold it always felt when I was standing dithering while I waited for the Police to pick me up. I say dithering from cold but I think some of it was due to feeling anxious or nervous about what was happening at home as I never knew what to expect upon my return. Chewing gum was another hazard in the Telephone Box and if you were lucky enough to avoid it sticking to your shoe then you were doing well although some people thought it funny to stick their discarded gum in all manner of places inside there.

Sometimes when I think about the village I feel torn as it does hold a soft spot in my heart. It was after all a lovely Rural Village where English Oak, Ash and Hazelnut trees dominated the landscape and provided us Kids with many tree swings, dens and hours of fun. Infact there was no end to our talents in den building and we really upped the ante one summer holiday by going all out for a whole new design with one of our camps by building it underground! A narrow tunnel was dug out creating an area which served as the entrance, leading from there we created a much larger area which again had been dug out so that it could provide space for all of the 'Gang' to fit in. The whole Camp was dug into the ground to a depth that could accommodate us in a comfortable sitting position and covered by wall to wall carpet which had been either begged or borrowed and lastly the roof which was constructed of scraps of wooden sheeting and timber which covered the roof area enabling us to make it as watertight as we could given the materials we had. Any leaks were swiftly obliterated with the aid of the odd polythene sheeting.

Our Village was a place where everyone knew each other and people took the time to speak to one another, a place that if you walked around you would be treading on Hopscotch chalked pavements and any small dips in the pavement would accommodate a game of Marbles; a place where if you left your bike out overnight it was in exactly the same place the next morning. Infact, everyone felt free in those days, even the dogs ran loose around the village and chalky white dog poo was a common hazard to avoid, that was at a time when we could feed our dogs bones, before Health and Safety this and Health and Safety that and definitely a time before poop scooping was even heard of.

The Villagers were always enthusiastic about making an event out of everything, "Bonfire Night" being a prime example and we started to build our "Bonnie" about two weeks before the 'Big Night' and I guess it provided a good service for the locals as it gave them the opportunity to discard of any household items that were no longer needed, either way I never heard of anyone in our village having to do a run to the Council Tip and, to be perfectly honest I am not sure whether or not the Council had a 'Tip' anyway. The Bonnie was always in the same place year after year, behind the street lamp at the very bottom of our cul-de-sac opposite our house on the grassed area which led onto the Playing Field. It was massive and we had great fun leading up to Bonfire Night by doing "Penny for the Guy". We used to sit outside the shops in the Precinct and do nothing short of beg for money off anyone going in or out of the shops. The money we collected was immediately divided up between us and we would go straight away into the Newsagent to buy sweets. When Bonfire Night finally arrived the Guy took on a new role and would take pride of place on the very top of the fire. After a responsible Grown Up lit the fire and the flames engulfed the Guy it was like saying goodbye to an old friend, after all we had spent a good two weeks carting it all over the place to plead for money. As the evening got underway we used to have toffee apples, homemade toffee, cinder toffee and jacket potatoes which were simply divine with a bit of Stork margarine in them and we were so keen to eat them that we could barely hold them in our hands because they were still piping hot. The morning afterwards we would still be able to find some *Taties which we had overlooked the night before. Fireworks were another huge part of the entertainment but I never really liked them as I always thought that there would be some major tragedy if one randomly blew up in someone's face so I used to participate in the celebration with the rather tamer handling of Sparklers and, to be honest, I wasn't very comfortable with them either. Everything about Bonfire Night was magical right down to the simplest of pleasures such as making footprints in the crisp, white frosty grass or blowing into the air and watching the heat from your breath appear. Happy days!!!

One Bonfire Night led to bitter disappointment and much sadness for me and it made me question my Mam's sanity, you see I had been desperate for some Wellington Boots as I had outgrown mine and all the other Kids were having the stylish black ones and I wanted a pair just to be like the other kids. One afternoon I returned home from School and Mam proudly produced a carrier bag with a surprise for me and as I took a peek inside the bag. I accidentally dropped the bag to the floor where my surprise proceeded to reveal itself ... A pair of luminous orange wellies revealed themselves! I thought my Mam was bloody insane, I was devastated and thought there was no way I would be wearing them as I would look like a right Numpty and all the Kids would make snide comments at me and taunt me. Before I knew it a large lump began to form in my throat and I ran from the room up to the privacy of my bedroom where I proceeded to cry my eyes out on my bed feeling that yet another dream was lost. It was just the same for us over gloves in winter because when it snowed Kelvin

* Taties – Geordie word for Potatoes.

and I were the only numpty's wearing socks with *Taties in on our hands instead of Mittens. Why, oh, why couldn't she just get us a pair of Bloody Gloves each? They would have cost less than two of her "Breakers", Breakers by the way are cans of strong Lager made by an American Company called Coors. We should have known then that we were not at the top of Mam's list of priorities!

Christmas time was yet again upon us and Carol Singing was another easy way of making money too. We used to gather in Gangs of about six and knock on the doors of a couple of streets before going to exchange our coppers for sweets, crisps or chocolate. This was a doddle to me as I used to mime to the songs and nobody was any the wiser and I can visualise myself now huddled in a small group under the street lamp where we used to share all the money out. Car Washing was another nice little earner, knocking on the neighbour's doors with a bucket and sponge and charging them a small fee for doing a rather inferior job if I was to be totally honest, mainly due to the fact that it was ok washing the car but we weren't very keen on the all-important rinsing of the vehicle which obviously would have finished the job off much better. As I said earlier to some degree the village was a dream place to live in for our little family that is before Dad left, afterwards it became a Prison as there didn't seem to be anywhere or anyone to run to for help to escape the misery and to be perfectly honest I didn't know who I could trust.

The village as it happened contained some beautiful Ancient Woodlands and Wildlife Surveys have since classified much of the area as an 'A' grade which means that it is 'An area of very high natural history, containing several varied habitats with a wide diversity of plants and animals'. In May 2009 an archaeological desk-based assessment was carried out where it identified an array of medieval to post medieval landscape components – fields of extant ridges and furrows, ponds

---

* Taties – Geordie word for holes.

and hedgerows surviving along boundaries shown on 18th Century maps, in other words, they found a pattern of ridges and troughs that had been created by a system of ploughing used in Europe during the Middle Ages. Now this information triggers something else in my memory ... after the Farmer had finished ploughing the field next to our house we always used to go and play there. During these times I have found so many Clay Tobacco Pipes which had been unearthed by the plough and wondered where they had come from. How I wish I had kept them, most were broken but there was the odd one that was still intact and I used to pretend I was smoking a pipe. As it happens, the use of Clay Pipes in Britain dates back to the 1580's and continued well into the early twentieth century once being very common in Europe peaking between 1850-1920, when after the Great War Cigarettes took over from the Pipe as they were much cheaper. I wonder which century my treasures came from. I have also found old coins but I couldn't even tell you what era they were from or where I put them much to my disappointment. It would have been amazing if they had been Roman coins. I wonder if you have heard of the Staffordshire Hoard which was found in early July 2009. An unemployed man was in his friend's field with a Metal Detector when he discovered the largest and most valuable hoard of gold and silver treasure in history when over 3500 pieces were unearthed and I am led to believe that the pieces recovered were dated back to Anglo-Saxon times making the treasure over 1300 years old.

Chapter 6

Sticklebacks and Jam Jars

During the years that I lived in the village I had a great friendship with my neighbours Irish Red Setter dog called Mowbray and their cat Yukky and many a time Mowbray has helped me out of a sticky situation with my Mam, you see, if I refused to eat my dinner Mam used to present the same meal to me for supper, breakfast and dinner the next day and so on, so I used to sneak Mowbray into our house and conceal him under the table where I proceeded to sneak him my food. He was always in trouble too for jumping into the Brook and getting dirty and smelly and his owners Camilla, Connor and Connor Jnr, who used to live next door but one to us, used to put old socks on his paws to try and deter him from doing this so it was only right that I returned the favour and took off his socks and let him loose on the brook which by the way had a rather distinct smell about it.

Our immediate neighbours who lived directly next door to us were Dafyyd Senior, Dafyyd Jnr and his wife Paula who I am pretty sure were originally from Wales; they had a baby girl and Kelvin and I got into trouble with Dafyyd Jnr for running up our stairs in the middle of the day and making too much noise, err hello I thought these three bedroomed houses were built for FAMILIES plus we can't have been making that much noise because our Dad worked shifts too therefore we would have been mindful not to disturb him while he slept.

Camilla and Connor were Mam and Dad's very best friends and I used to spend loads of time around at their house talking to Camilla, who I liked a lot. She sprang into action and came to my rescue one day when I got stung by a Wasp whilst I was playing inside her Frame Tent. It went up my trouser leg and stung me. My Mam could hear me screaming from our house which was two doors down. How I loved those trousers, they were a deep purple colour with a flare and were certainly different than any other trousers I had ever seen as they had a bright red Dragon embroidered onto the top half of them above my knee going all the way up to my front pocket.

I was mesmerised with something else at Camilla's which was a real Ostrich egg that they had brought back from their travels. I thought Duck Eggs were big but they were nowhere near the size of an Ostrich egg. After spending many hours studying this egg I came to the conclusion that something was really bothering me about it ... how did it fit through the birds bum when it was time for the bird to lay? Camilla and Connor also had a Salmon coloured American style fridge which I was fascinated with, our white Ariston one was a top of the range but I had never seen one that big before or that colour Wow! They also had the most beautiful gardens and took great pride in them; everything was pristine including the stripes that were on the lawn right up to the wood stain on the shed.

I remember that Dad had to return to the North-East for some reason and Mam was invited out for a drink with Connor and Camilla while he was away and they all decided to go to the Club, which I think was nice of them to think about my Mam being on her own. Dad and Mam were able to return the favour when Connor had to go into Hospital and they invited Camilla out for the evening, all was well until all four of them met up again and went out to the Club and this is where my Brother said that the following happened (in his words) "That sick and twisted Pig did her usual dwelling on nothing and made it into something", She made a huge scene by saying that our Dad had paid for more drinks with Camilla than what Connor had done with her! Dad was so embarrassed at Mam's outburst and it made it really difficult for the friendship to survive after that and as such things were never the same again between them. Kelvin also said that when Dad left, Mam lost all of their good friends, all the nice people, and ended up hanging around with the shite from the village and it was common knowledge that the Villagers couldn't wait to see the back of her. I can't explain in words how bad she was but she was truly appalling and it seemed that she had no shame with whatever she did to the point where she used to take Kelvin and me to sleep over at her friend Betty's house which was more or less opposite to The Raven. Betty had loads of Kids and the house was strikingly dirty, infact it was filthy and Kelvin and I would have to bunk in bed with her Kids while Mam and Betty went to the Pub. The beds were filthy too as was the Kitchen and the toilet which had the most intense smell of urine I have ever smelt and to make matters worse Betty was openly stealing electricity from the next door neighbours house while they were away on their holiday, I know this because she had the electric cooker propped up on an old beer crate so that she could rewire the shortened electric cable back into the cooker socket on the wall plus she had an electricity cable going from her back door over into the neighbour's house. I wasn't too sure that the rig up she had made in order to do this was very safe and half expected her house to go up in flames with me and my Brother in it!

Mam was not the only character in the village; there was Dancing Davy who was a very tall black man who was always smiling and laughing and he used to dance around with us Kids, we always felt like he was a fun person to be around.

Old Cleggy was another character who liked the drink infact I don't recall ever seeing him sober. Old Cleggy's gable end used to face my friend's Mia's gable end and as such their back doors were facing one another, this had an advantage for Mia as Cleggy's Son, who was in his mid-thirties and had what I now know to be a Severe Learning Difficulty, liked to watch everyone in the street from his bedroom window and it was when we were standing at the back door of Mia's house one afternoon along with our other friend Mia's next door neighbour Jodie that Mia did the unthinkable ... I was busy standing at her back door munching on a raw carrot which I was dipping into Mia's sugar bowl when she caught sight of Cleggy's Son and lifted her top up and started flashing her boobs at him, well he went bananas and the more he went bananas the more she did it. It wasn't like he could talk so instead he used to make loud noises and I can remember thinking at the time that she was really bad and to top it all she was supposed to be a good girl especially as she attended the local Catholic school and not forgetting all the Church Services that she supposedly attended, God she was brave, I wouldn't have dared plus even at my age I knew full well that this was not the right way to behave.

Another day we were playing near the prefabricated garage blocks which were situated at the top of the village near Shakespeare Avenue when some Lads came past, they boldly broke into one of the garages where there just so happened to be a mattress in there and somehow Mia decided to entertain them with sexual favours of some description (not sure what they were as I was far too young, besides which I didn't know what sex was) but the Lads were lining up outside the garage only to come out boasting to one another about Tit's and Fanny's. After about half an hour had passed Mia came out of the garage and turned on me rather smugly and asked me "Are you a virgin"? Well I hadn't a clue what she was asking and to hide my embarrassment and lack of knowledge in this area I rather foolishly responded with "Don't be so stupid"! I can honestly say that the only good thing that came from that situation was that thankfully my Brother was not one of the Lads in the queue.

Old Cleggy and my Dad had a run in once and as Dad was as a man of few words it made the incident even more comical. Dad was walking Charlie late one night, that's our dog which I told you about earlier, when Cleggy threw a glass bottle across the road at Charlie which luckily didn't hit him but smashed close by to him. Anyway, Dad swiftly responded by following Cleggy to his house who by now was safely inside, Dad knocked on the front door and Cleggy answered just as he had anticipated. Dad decided to say very little preferring instead to punch Cleggy just the once straight in the mouth breaking his false teeth in the process and leaving the poor bloke flat on his back on the Hallway floor. By the time Cleggy came to he was still quite dazed and must have been quite bewildered I'm sure. Strangely enough, Cleggy had quite a responsible job at the Pit; he was in charge of sending the men down in the Cage to the Rock Face phew! God only knows how he maintained this role with him being the village drunk. It's a wonder there wasn't a tragedy of some kind.

Further up the road from Mia and Jodie was my other friend Bonnie who originally came from Wales. Kelvin seems to recall her being Spanish and I was wondering if maybe Bonnie's Mum was Spanish and Dad Welsh. This is why I am confused about her origins because I think we all used to call her Dad Blackie (no idea why) she had an older Brother called Godofredo who I recall was serving in the Army. I can remember meeting him when he was at home on leave; he was always nice to his Mum and kind to Bonnie. Hmm now I think about it the strange thing is that we used to play together loads of the time but can't ever remember us all playing together with Jodie and Mia (not sure why) as Kids just mingled in with one another without questions being asked, everybody being the same and on an equal footing which I suppose was par for the course living in a Pit village, as most Pit Villages nationwide were esoteric in nature.

As with all communities came triumph and heartbreak with the latter being one that I wish I could forget, unfortunately this is not the case therefore I shall tell you about the incident with the Ice Cream Van. The Ice Cream Man was on his rounds and had stopped at the top of the road just outside Auntie Penny's house when all of a sudden a chaotic situation presented, well it was more like a noisy commotion ... I ran as fast as my legs could take me to the top of the cul-de-sac to see what all the fuss was about and upon my arrival it was clear to see that something very serious had happened ... after scanning the immediate area for a few seconds I then located the source of all the commotion. It was my little friend Maddie who was lying still in the middle of the road, there was blood trickling from her head onto the tarmac where it began to form a small puddle. Suddenly hushed tones encompassed the scene and I saw her older Brother Declan arrive with their Dad who also happened to be on leave from the Army. Maddie was a couple of years younger than me and I think she would have been about 6 at the time, Declan being about 7 or 8. It soon transpired that Maddie had done what all Kids are warned by their Parents not to do, she stepped out from the back of the ice cream van in order to try and cross over to the other side of the road and that was when the car hit her. It was heart breaking seeing their Dad pick one of her shoes up and put it into his trouser pocket; you see she only had one shoe on by now as the other had been flung off into the middle of the road with the force of the impact. Her Dad was crouched over her and sobbing like a baby just rocking back and forth all the time, even to me it was clear to see that the situation looked quite hopeless as he picked his limp little girl up and cradled her to his chest, his beautiful little dark haired, olive skinned Daughter was dead. For months after this tragedy the village seemed to retreat into numbness to the point where if I was to be honest I don't think that any of us knew how to deal with the situation and it appeared to me that Maddie's family certainly weren't coping. They just appeared to carry a shadow of grief and sorrow around with them. Everyone understood their reactions and no one could blame the family or criticise them after all how does anyone come to terms with losing their child?

Now I mentioned earlier that my Brother and I were arch enemies and battle began first thing in a morning until last thing at night, what I didn't mention was the time when I found my Brother being circled in the corn field by a gang of boys who were dead set on bashing him up. I was on my way back home via the very same field as I had been to play with some friends from further up the village. I soon became aware of the situation as I quickly made my way towards my Brother and managed to push my way through the middle of the boys into the centre of the gang where I managed to stand back to back with my Brother ready to take them on. The first punch was thrown pretty quickly following a verbal onslaught and a few kicks here and there for good measure all the while thinking that there was no way I was going to let anyone get the better of either of us, time seemed to pass slowly during all the action and it was only when I briefly paused to check on my Brother that I discovered that in all the chaos he was nowhere to be seen ... Chicken!!!!! I still to this day do not know what the fight was about. The very same corn field became the scene of probably one of my Brother's biggest crimes. Apparently he was out playing with his friends when he said that they dared him to pinch some matches out of a car that a man was washing at the time, so Kelvin spied his chance and when the chap went to get more water he made his move, mission accomplished! It wasn't long afterwards that holy hell broke loose in our house and the village which resulted in my Brother being stripped naked by our Mam and being "belted" half to death. He was then kept under house arrest and confined to his bedroom for two days to the point where even I felt sorry for him. It later transpired that the gang had decided to pick some corn on the cob out of the field and light a fire so that they could cook it; this decision was a really disastrous one as it resulted in a major incident as the whole cornfield went up in flames and three cul-de-sacs including ours ended up being evacuated as the blaze ravished the surrounding farmland, needless to say that the Farmer failed to harvest a crop of corn that year and Kelvin and I you will be pleased to know, never ever played with matches again ...

Unfortunately, this was not the last time a Fire Engine visited our property, infact I can recall two more incidents which were fairly serious ... The first one was when Mia, Kelvin and I arrived home to an empty house and we were starving hungry so Mia being Mia suggested that we fry some chips and that was where the problem started, you see, she was a couple of years older than me and far more experienced in the catering department so out came the chip pan ready to warm the lard up. I was peeling the taties and Kelvin was busy spreading Stork margarine on the bread ready for the chip butties. I can't remember whether it was Kelvin or Mia that loaded the chips into the sizzling hot fat but in they went along with a very large quantity of cold, starchy water and that was when pandemonium broke out. The scene in the Scullery looked more like a scene from the film Backdraft with the whole area going up in flames, Kelvin and I did the only decent thing that we could think of and ran into the garden feeling absolutely terrified leaving Mia to do her firefighting alone which she attempted with the aid of a soaking wet tea towel. Needless to say that it wasn't long before the local Fire Brigade joined us along with Mam! Her beautiful sparkling white Scullery was destroyed and we were in the shit BIGTIME!

The second incident I will tell you about later ...

One of my favourite pastimes was going to the local pond along with my friends. We were always fully equipped for the trip with fishing nets and jam jars that we had adapted with a temporary handle which we had crafted from some garden string. On our arrival we would walk along a rotten and diseased tree that just so happened to have fallen horizontally half way across the pond. The pond was green and smelly with algae and it seemed to be the perfect environment for the Sticklebacks and Tadpoles, probably due to the fact that it was surrounded by mature trees which provided a lot of shade. The art of walking across the tree was a treacherous thing to do at the best of times and was similar to walking on a tight rope but the manoeuvre became even trickier to undertake if I met Kelvin and his friends up there as there always seemed to be a scuffle mid-way on the log when we tried to pass one another. Now for me this would have been a recipe for disaster if I had fallen in as I couldn't swim, infact, I am ashamed to say it but I didn't learn to swim until I was 12 years old, something I blame entirely on my Brother as he terrorised me when Mam and Dad took us to the 50 metre Olympic sized swimming pool in the City Centre. He had great pleasure in going under the water and pretending to tug me underneath where I felt for sure that I was going to drown, my response to this was to cling to the side of the pool with my fingers gripping tightly to the tiled gulley's which were around the edge of the pool and where I used to end up facing for what seemed like hours. If Kelvin came anywhere near me I would instantly cry and scream so you can imagine that swimming trips were not something that I relished as it just meant that I would always without fail end up being one stage away from hypothermia as I dared not to move away from the relative safety of the pool side. On hearing the inevitable commotion Dad always used to come to my rescue and pick me up, hold me close, well as close as he could considering that I was wearing a rubber ring and armbands and gently talk to me in order to calm me down and reassure me. I also remember wearing the most ridiculous navy blue swimming costume which had a white lace pretend skirt bit attached to it which I think I inherited from my Cousin Dionne and which I felt like a total numpty in. My Brother however learnt to swim in a totally different environment which as it turns out was definitely a case of either "sink or swim", you see our local High School had an outdoor swimming pool area which was encompassed by six foot slatted wooden fencing and where particularly over the big summer holidays all the local kids would scale the fence and congregate, there was only one problem with this and that was that the older kids tended to throw the youngsters into the pool regardless of whether they could swim or not and as it happens Kelvin was one of those youngsters who unfortunately could not swim so rather than drown he had the sense to try and stay calm and have a go at this swimming lark which everyone raved about. He was successful and that is the story of how my Brother learnt to swim.

One of my Brother's hobbies was Oology which is the collecting of wild bird eggs. All the lads in the village seemed to be doing it and would boast about their collections. There was a nice little group of them that would do swapsies and their collections were proudly displayed in discarded shoeboxes which were carefully labelled, lined with cotton wool and placed tentatively in the boxes. Eggs as it happens will rot if the contents are left inside for any length of time and must therefore be 'blown' in order to remove their contents, this was done by putting a tiny pin hole at the top and bottom of the egg and a person blowing with their mouth into the egg to force the contents out, thankfully this hobby did not last too long with Kelvin which I'm pleased about particularly as the Wild Birds Protection Act 1954 and Wildlife and Countryside Act 1981 has made it impossible to collect wild bird's eggs legally so my naughty Brother and his friends shouldn't have been doing it. At a similar time another horrid craze of the lads was to blow frogs up; apparently this involved a straw being put up the frogs bum and a person blowing air into it to the point of explosion. I thought this was disgusting and cruel and hoped that my Brother was not one of the culprits and if you are reading this Kelvin then please do not tell me either way as I would rather not know.

The only birthday party I can remember having was when I was about 8 years old and it was a blazing hot summer's day during the big six week summer holidays, I was wearing a navy blue pair of shorts, matching sports vest and red flip flops and Mam was in good spirits so much so that even the paddling pool was out in the garden for all of us to play in, we had a great afternoon playing 'pass the parcel' and 'musical chairs'. The next morning before I went to school I went out to take a look in the garden only to find that my pool was overrun by these horrid black looking creatures that I had never seen before and had absolutely no idea what they were. After seeking advice it transpired that the mysterious creatures were infact Newts. I had never seen a Newt before but can remember I was not impressed as I thought that they looked pretty gross. My Brother on the other hand thought it would be a great idea to put one in a jam jar and take it to school where he proudly showed the rest of the pupils his exhibit and where I avoided him for the rest of the day. Sadly birthdays were never special after Dad had gone, with little or no fuss being made by Mam, at best we received a windbreaker sized card and a bag of Ket, Ket by the way is another northern name for cheap and nasty sweets, penny chews like black jacks, fruit salads and bubbly gums. I never really took much notice of what Kelvin had for his birthday until a particular year when Dad decided to buy him a Gat Air Pistol which was a British made gun designed by a chap called T J Harrington & Co Ltd it could fire .177 pellets, ball bearings, darts and corks and guess which one Kelvin threatened to always "get me with"? Darts! Other Harrington products around the time were the 'Ding Dong' slingshot and the 'Little Kraka' fishing reel. I'm really not sure if he had any of these other gadgets but I do remember him making some slingshots out of a 'Y' shaped branch, elastic and piece of leather, I think most Boys of a similar age had already learnt the skill of making these at quite a young age.

Chapter 7

The Pit

The Colliery that Dad worked at began operating in 1917 and was situated at the top of the village, as soon as you saw the Pit you became aware of the dangerous environment you were stepping into due to all the hustle and bustle that was constant.

As a result of the Colliery a new settlement grew up and many new houses were built by the mining company, the standards at the time they were built were quite good and quite impressive; they had inside toilets which was unusual for working class housing at that time. Conditions at the Mines had also improved and some had Pit Baths as early as the 1920's, the ones that didn't had to wait until 1947 and if you were one of the unfortunate ones not to have this facility then a Miner would return to his family home after a shift and the Wife would boil the water ready to fill the tin bath, the Father would then have his bath infront of the coal fire.

The Pit Baths were where Miner's had a "clean locker" and a "dirty locker" and each were located in different parts of the baths. Miner's would leave their ordinary clothes in the "clean locker" and change into their work clothes ready for the shift 720 yards underground. After the shift had finished the Miner would leave his work clothes in the "dirty locker" where they would be dried by hot air which was constantly blowing through the lockers ready for his next shift. I can remember Dad having certain clothes that he used to wear to and from his shift as he was mindful not to ruin any of his good clothes. Our Pit was fortunate enough to have a Social Club which was built in 1924 and remained open until 2012. It also had a Medical Centre which was located next to the Pit Baths and Canteen. Nationalisation on the 1st January 1947 meant that the Colliery became part of the National Coal Board (NCB) and as such Health and Safety procedures improved with proper Medical Centres being built. Most hours were spent treating day-to-day cuts, bruises and strains that Miner's had suffered. However, at times they had to care for Miner's who had been seriously injured underground and during one of these times we lost my Great Uncle Edwin in a Pit Fall at this very same Pit. If he had only worked his usual shift he would have been safe at home when the disaster struck, instead he was working overtime so that he could provide his family with some extra income. He was one of three men killed that day and the only saving grace was that he did not suffer as Pit Officials said that he was killed instantly. The unexpected and tragic loss of my Uncle Edwin left my Great Auntie Penny and her three children Edwin Jnr, Jeffrey and Chrissy devastated. I can't remember my Uncle Edwin but my Granda Edgar's Sister Penny was a lovely lady, she was the only girl to six Brothers, George, James, Lesley, Joel, Charlie and my Granda Edgar. I loved spending time with her, they lived in the next cul-de-sac to ours and had a lovely Golden Retriever called Max who was a big softy.

Now getting back to the Pit, I feel it's important that you understand the Community and how they always united and pulled together particularly when tragic times presented so much so that when there was a disaster the villagers would gather at the Pit Gates waiting for news of their loved ones. It became a place where time dragged, emotions ran high and the village united to support one another. Recently Dad's old Pit featured on Central News marking the 30th Anniversary of the Miners' Strike; even though the Pit and Social Club are long gone the spirit of the Community is as intense as ever, it's hard to believe that the time has gone so quickly. The Strike in 1984 was different than the two that had taken place in the 70's where the Miner's won pay increases. This strike was about jobs after it was announced that twenty Pits were to be closed resulting in the potential loss of 20,000 jobs. Various Pits decided to strike and on the 12th March 1984 Arthur Scargill, President of the NUM (National Union of Mineworkers) called for the strike to become a national strike and during this very challenging time the Community really pulled together. At first, they thought it would only be a matter of weeks and then the men would be back to work, but it lasted almost a year. The Miners' Wives joined forces and began with Soup Kitchens so that they could feed everyone. It's hard to believe that in modern times hunger was a very real issue, I don't say that lightly, kids were starving so they pulled what they could together and accepted food donations from whoever they could so that they could at least provide one hot meal a day to each family member. Looking back it must have been incredibly difficult to cope with the emotions after sending the children to bed hungry but there wasn't anything they could do. Some of the protest banners seen on the television during the strike said "Stealing the bread out of our kid's mouths". The strike could never have happened without the women's groups, on the picket lines, facing immense brutality and sexual harassment from the Police who called them "Scargill's Slags". These brave women marched, campaigned, collected money and picketed alongside their men, just bear in mind that this was something that had never happened before in a Pit Strike and not long after this the Mines were privatised in 1987 and the Colliery closed in 1991. The Social Club became a large part of all our lives with everyone in the village joining in on the Annual Village Carnival which was held every year up until the Miner's Strike of 1984. Weddings were always something that all the villagers got involved with and there was nothing better for us kids than chasing the wedding float which was actually a coal delivery lorry 'done up to the nines' with the Bride and Groom sitting on throne like chairs on the flatbed trailer at the back, here they would scatter handfuls of coppers onto the streets for the children to scramble for.

I don't think my Mam and Dad ever went to the pub then. They were members of the Club you see, which meant that social evenings were much more structured and Pie and Pea Suppers, Dinner Dances and themed evenings were always on the social calendar. Dad had a Burton's Menswear account and took great pride in his wardrobe, often wearing a new sports jacket, suit or something else. He always looked 'champion' and I remember Mam bought a sleeveless black cat suit which had a mock gold chain belt and pleated culottes' style legs for one of the social evenings. She always looked nice when she was going out and used to make a huge effort with her hair, nails and make-up, even with all the effort it still didn't stop her from causing a whole load of grief for Dad when they were out which often involved others and nearly always caused a massive argument. It got to the point that if I saw Mam wearing her headscarf and heated rollers I would start to feel really anxious because that was a sign that she was going to be going out for the night and it always felt to me that she didn't seem to have much patience with us which meant that she would be quite quick tempered and as such you could bet your bottom dollar that it usually resulted in us having a smack at some point during the day.

Some of my fondest memories are of my Dad finishing his night shift at the Pit and coming to pick me up and taking me back to the Pit Canteen where we would have a thick, white canteen mug of strong tea and bacon butty for breakfast, even today a bacon and tomato ketchup sandwich is my idea of heaven ...

My Dad worked shifts and because of this we must have been the only family in the cul-de-sac that had a letterbox knocker with a pair of tights bound around it so that it wouldn't wake Dad if someone tried to knock on the front door, thankfully this didn't happen often as in those days everyone who knew you would use the back door and it would only be official visitors that would use the front door.

Dad used to take his Bait to work in a Sunblest or Mother's Pride bread wrapper, and more often than not he would open a tin of Pek Ham to have on his sandwiches, traditionally a Miner's bait was a simple meal of water and bread and jam as no Miner would eat much underground as the crouching position that they worked in was the main cause of heartburn. I am sure my Granda Edgar used to take his bait in a metal tin so that he could deter the rats from eating his bait, I never heard my Dad mention any rats, I did however ask him where the toilet facilities were once you were underground and the answer ... I'll leave to your own imagination.

Another memory of my Dad was when he used to finish his shift and return home and lie on his stomach on the living room floor and after taking his T shirt off he would ask me to sit on his back and with the aid of a metal hair grip he would ask me to extract the pieces of coal dust that had got embedded into the skin on his back, the hair grip would be a cruder version of a modern day comedone extractor and as it happens I quite liked doing this as it felt quite therapeutic plus it never failed to fascinate me how after putting a tiny bit of pressure on the loop end of the hair grip it would force the coal to 'pop out' and therefore be removed.

I think that it is important that you know how much Dad was respected in our community so much so that when he finally made the decision to return to the North-East he put his notice in at the Pit where I think it was the norm to work three or four weeks' notice, however after doing so, the Foreman/Deputy approached Dad and was very sympathetic to his situation and told him to just work a couple of days and then get himself away from Mam as quick as he could but by doing this Kelvin thinks that Dad actually broke his contract with the Pit which makes us both wonder if it had any effect on his Redundancy Package or his Pit Pension in later years.

'The Durham Miners' Gala' is a large annual gathering that is held on the second Saturday in July in Durham City Centre and is associated with the coal mining heritage and particularly that of the Miners' Trade Unionism of Durham Coalfield, which stretched throughout the traditional County of Durham. Some people call it "The Big Meeting" or "Durham Big Meeting", Dad has attended every year since he moved back to the North-East and I am led to believe that it's a great day out for all the family.

The main assembly point is the City Centre Market Place and Bands and Banners start to March from there to the Racecourse from 8.30am, each Banner is typically accompanied by a Brass Band and when they reach their destination political speeches are delivered. In the afternoon a Miners' Service is held in Durham Cathedral which may include the blessing of any new Banners. The first Union was established in 1869 and the first Gala was held in 1871 at Wharton Park, Durham, from there it developed into the largest unofficial Miners' and Trade Union gathering in the UK and attracted over 300,000 people which is actually seven times the population of Durham City. Banners are taken on foot from each Colliery into Durham and the event is marked by large Unions of men marching on the roads leading into the City. The Gala was only cancelled from 1915-18 due to the First World War, 1921, 1922 and 1926 all due to Strikes and again from 1940-45 due to the Second World War and the effect of the 1984-85 Strike also led to the Gala being called off in 1984. My Dad has always said that there is always a lovely atmosphere to the day and if you think about it it is quite amazing that this event is as important today as it was back in 1871.

The Jarrow March or (Jarrow Crusade) is another historical event that happened in October 1936. It was a Protest March against unemployment and I can remember my Granda Edgar talking about this, it was to protest about the extreme poverty suffered in the North-East during the Great Depression, 207 Marchers travelled from Jarrow to the Palace of Westminster in London, a journey covering 300 miles on foot to lobby Parliament. Their MP was Ellen Wilkinson also known as 'Red Ellen' who walked alongside the men but sadly when they completed their feat, very little was done to improve the situation for them and the Town's Shipbuilding industry remained closed and the Marchers were given the £1 each train fare to get back home. During the 19th and 20th Centuries its main industries were iron and steel for Shipbuilding and a collapse in orders during the Great Depression led to its closure in 1933 leaving unemployment levels at 72.9% which I personally think is shocking. It was remarkable what the Marchers did considering that they only had a good set of boots which had been donated by the public and the goodwill of locals during their journey that offered them food and shelter for the night. It took them almost a month to make the journey and they presented a petition with 11,000 signatures on, still no proposal was made to help the people of Jarrow. The March by the way is the subject of the songs "Marshall Riley's Army" by Lindisfarne and "Jarrow Song" by Alan Price. The March was a remarkable act of determination and community spirit during an immensely difficult time and although very little was done to assist the people of Jarrow, it shows a determination for the people to "stand up and be counted" for what they truly believed in.

I am currently researching my Family Tree and am hoping that I will uncover a connection to the great Shipbuilders of the North-East. I feel it is so important to know who I am, where I came from and to learn about my heritage so that I can pass this information onto my Son.

Chapter 8

I don't like Mondays – (The Boomtown Rats)

Kelvin and I attended the local Infant and Middle schools which were built around 1954, the High School followed sometime afterwards. Kelvin used to taunt me by saying that when students started the High School they would be thrown into the outdoor swimming pool which I mentioned earlier, this was supposedly some kind of 'initiation', the sheer thought of this terrified me and much to my relief I didn't have to go there as we moved.

My mind is now wandering and thoughts of my early school days bring back a lot of memories such as the outdoor toilet blocks which were a great hiding place. The building was crudely built with concrete blocks and the roof was constructed using corrugated sheeting, the floor was also concrete and had a channel built into the floor that acted as an overspill area for mopping out or any flooding, this ran down one side of the building underneath the wash hand basins. The smell from the toilets was unforgettable, not from being unclean; it just smelled damp even in the summer as there was no source of heating and once inside the toilets the light was very poor due to the small windows which were very high up. Everyone knew who was going for a 'Poo' as the Dinner Lady on Playground Duty would carry a role of izal toilet paper around and if you needed to go she used to rip you some sheets off. The sheer thought of everyone knowing 'my business' must have scarred me for life as I have always had an aversion to doing a number 2 in public toilets. "What time is it Mr Wolf" and playing 'Tick' are all great memories for me as I was a fast runner which meant I tended to have a better advantage than some of the other kids. I met my very first boyfriend, Neil, at Infant School and even though he had an overshot jaw I thought he was just gorgeous. We used to sit on the playground wall holding hands with one another, infact nobody else got a look in during our little romance. People used to call Neil a B***ard but his Mum Carla told him that his Dad had died in the War before he was born and it wasn't until many years later that I worked out what the underlying suggestion was. My next boyfriend was a tall, blonde lad with freckles called Robin and he lived with his family in the middle of the village. I didn't really go out with Robin for too long as I can remember that when I kissed him he always used to taste of something odd ... Similar to strawberry flavoured yoghurt and I wasn't so keen after that plus to be fair he did have rather large front teeth which I kind of compensated for by reassuring myself that although they were large at least they were dazzlingly white and clean although really there was no compensating for the kiss itself as I can still feel the force of my front teeth clashing with his, perhaps this was not my best idea afterall.

It was while I was at Infant School that I was proud to hold the superior position of "Milk Monitor". This position had a massive bonus ... nobody but nobody messed with the Milk Monitor! Free milk (one third of a pint) was introduced in schools after World War II to try and compensate for vitamin deficiencies following food rationing during and after the war.

I absolutely adored milk and loved this part of my school day even when the months were warmer and the milk was served at room temperature.

In the 70's it was felt by the Conservative Government that we no longer needed this as health had improved considerably over the years and as such Margaret Thatcher was dubbed: "Mrs Thatcher, the school milk snatcher", something that haunted her throughout her Career and in 1985 it cost her an Honorary Degree from Oxford University because of her Education Cuts and just to make matters worse there was also during this time some controversy regarding the allocation of Free School Dinners to the poor kids either way both issues made National News.

During these early school years of mine all Pupils were summoned to the Headmistress's room to read to her once a week as part of the 'Key Words Reading Scheme' which is a Series of 36 English Language early readers children's books which were published by the British publishing Company, Ladybird Books. The first book in the Series was published in 1964 and was completed by the first publication of the 36th book in 1967, the year I was born. Starting with book 1a, children aged from 3 to 5 years old were introduced to the main characters, who were Brother and Sister Peter and Jane, and they had a dog called Pat and each story would tell you about their Mummy and Daddy, trips to the beach or the shops, rides on trains and buses etc. I remember practising "Here is Peter", "Peter is here", "Here is Jane", "Jane is here", "I like Peter", "I like Jane" and so on ... I didn't like reading to the Headmistress though as I used to be scared of her. She was a rather plump lady who was quite stern in her demeanour and reminds me now of the character 'Miss Agatha Trunchball' (the Trunchball) in Roald Dahl's book Matilda which is also a film that was released in 1996.

It was during my early school years that I undertook my first acting role and played the part of the Lead Dancer in the

Christmas Nativity Play. Weeks and weeks of practice and dress rehearsals took place leading up to the week just before the Christmas Holidays. I was feeling fairly confident about my part as I had practiced and practiced my part over and over again and felt that I could handle the very important part of leading the line of Dancers out onto the stage. Finally my 'moment of glory' arrived and my dancing had improved no end to the point where my body flowed to the music of the "Dance of the Seven Veils", this dance is usually described as danced by Salome and is one of the elaborations on the biblical tale of the execution of Joel the Baptist. The purpose of the dance was to inflame King Herod who infact was actually my Boyfriend Neil; he was supposed to be playing the part with incestuous desire. Opening night arrived before I knew it, well it was opening afternoon actually ... my moment had arrived and I was raring to go, I floated out onto the stage exactly just as I had rehearsed until ... I caught site of my Mam out of the corner of my eye, she was wearing a distinctive pea green coloured Mac type coat and was sitting on the front row of our gymnasium benches. She was following my every move and was laughing, well that was it, and you'd have thought that I had Rigor Mortis because it went downhill from there on and I hate to admit it but I had the worst case of stage fright you could ever imagine. Since that awful winters afternoon I never attempted to willingly sing or dance in public again apart from when Mam has tried to drag me onto the dance floor when we were either at family weddings or out at the local Club after she'd had a few too many Gold Label Barley Wines.

Unfortunately, this young experience of acting had a 'knock on' effect on me so much so that I hate to say it but I think I must have a phobia of performing in public. It is also fair to say at this point that I have never dyed my hair which people think is strange because my hair started to turn grey when I was only 16 years old and wearing make-up is another big no, no for me as growing up with my Mam and her choosing to go through all the rigmarole with both make-up and hair dye put me off for life. My second embarrassing 'freeze' memory was when my Mam entered me into a Fancy Dress Competition which the local Council Playscheme was hosting and I was not a happy bunny as she made me up into a Gypsy with a headscarf, large hoop clip on earrings and I was heavily made up with far too much make-up for my liking. If only you could have seen my face you would have known that I was not happy infact I clung to the back of my Mam's legs the minute it was my turn to parade infront of the audience. It was a God awful time and I remember feeling absolutely distraught by the whole thing and it didn't make an ounce of difference to me when my Mam tried to pull me away from her leg that I was clinging onto infact she was getting more and more annoyed with me and told me to "Stop being such a silly little girl".

When I married some years later I really struggled to take to the dance floor in order to perform the "First Dance" with my new Husband. I did manage to do it but felt so incredibly self-conscious about the whole thing and I must admit that I had been dreading the moment for months leading up to the Big Day just worrying myself silly that I wouldn't be able to go through with it and what if I lost my nerve.

Back to the story around the time of the school play ... Mam had got a part time cleaning job at my Brother's Junior School and she used to take me along with her when she was due in for her shift. I always remember her leaving me in the Art Room with lots of paper and colouring pencils and I always had a lovely time drawing copious amounts of pictures and writing short little stories. I was a good girl for my Mam and never wandered off or messed with anything that I shouldn't have and on her return we used to take the short cut home through the Gulley's, across the Park and over the Playing Field. Mam didn't actually need to work as we were more than comfortable financially but I think that she just wanted to earn some money of her own plus it helped to stop her from becoming bored at home.

Dad used to give Kelvin and I Tuck Shop money to take to school, he had this funny little trick of holding a Tuppence in one hand and a Shilling in the other and me being the little one always used to choose the biggest coin until one day I went for the silver coin and then all became equal. How I loved having my 'Tuck Money' as it meant that I could buy my favourite 'Cheese Puffs' or 'Cheese Snaps' from the Tuck Shop.

When my turn finally came for me to move up to Junior School my life became hell, which was very sad as school had become my haven and a place of safety. My Maths Teacher was Miss Bradshaw and she was short in height, had long blonde hair that was parted down the centre and had an annoying habit of always picking the loose hair off her clothing when she spoke to us. She was the problem because I used to have Maths four out of the five days of the week and I was terrified of her because she was very strict and in my opinion was far too nasty to be a Teacher, this meant that I spent most of the time too frightened to ask for help particularly when I was trying to get my head around Decimals and Fractions and so the top and bottom of it was that Tuesdays were the only day of the school week that I was happy and that was because I didn't have a lesson with Miss Bradshaw, How Bloody sad is that! In the last year of juniors my Class had Sex Education lessons. There had been a massive change in Sex Education due to the social changes of the 1960's and 70's to the point where even Biology text books provided fuller accounts of the Human Reproductive System and methods of Contraception were being taught more widely. The whole aim of the specialist lessons was to decrease any anxiety, embarrassment or issues to do with relationships, the only thing with that is that it was wasted on my Class as we were only interested in the bit about Pubic Lice ... Following our Sex Education lessons all the girls in my Class including myself thought it would be a great idea to wear two tennis balls up our vests and pretend we had Boobs, we used to mince around the back of the bike sheds pretending to be all grown up, this little fad went on for a few weeks until my chest began to get sore and I discovered hard lumps behind each nipple where the tennis balls had aggravated my flat chest, this was probably down to the fact that everyone used to try to grab them especially the boys who pretended to get a good handful of Boob ... Boys!

During the same year Jane who was in my Class had started her Periods. I only know this because there was a big fuss going on in the girls toilets when I went in to use the toilet (number 1 only) and I was invited along with others to look under the cubicle door, I had no idea why but went along with the request all the same even though I was about to regret the decision ... Jane was messing with the lower part of her clothing around her 'private bits' where she proceeded to demonstrate a rather crude effort of changing a Dr White Sanitary Towel which was attached to a Sanitary Belt, the group were awestruck but all I can remember is feeling horrified as I thought that all the blood I could see was serious and she had infact broken her tiddly. The other reason I was horrified was that there didn't seem to be any shame with Jane and I completely changed my view of her from that day on for the simple reason that if she could be so indiscreet about something that personal then there was no way I was going to share anymore of my secrets with her again.

I absolutely adored Sports Day and took part in all the Races finding particular strength in the Running races, Egg and Spoon and Skipping races. I never returned home without a handful of 1st or 2nd place certificates and it was at one of these Sports Days that I had what I now know to be a touch of anxiety, I don't know where it came from or what triggered it but I can recall looking along the Tracks to the sea of Parents who were sitting on the wooden benches spectating and cheering their Kids on and I began wondering why I was the only one in my Class without their Mam cheering them on. I felt lost for the first time in my life and Sports Days were never the same afterwards, even Kelvin had moved up to the High School so he wasn't there, which I guess would have been better than no one at all.

Hmm, another memory of Sports Day springs to mind and that is of the cheap little canvas Pumps we used to wear. In the

UK Plimsolls otherwise known as Pumps were compulsory in schools for Physical Education lessons and Kelvin and I used to wear either the black or white ones with the choice of either slip on or laced. These little Pumps were readily available in most of the local shops and were a type of athletic shoe with a canvas upper and rubber sole and were originally developed as Beachwear in the 1830's by the Liverpool Rubber Company. Unfortunately, they had another use at school too, as they were commonly used for Corporal Punishment, in plain terms 'getting the pump' was always something to dread. Thankfully the worst punishment I had at school was Detention and that was only once and to be honest even that wasn't my fault, yes, yes, I can hear you saying "Yeah right" but truly it wasn't, it was because my Best Friend Polly copied my History homework and once she had handed it in to Mr Stones we were both summoned to "see him after class", we had been rumbled! And so we stood side by side in the classroom after the history lesson had ended and Mr Stones said to us both "One of you has copied from the other, now who is going to admit to it"? We both stood silent "If the Culprit does not admit it then you are both in Detention" and because Polly failed to admit that it was infact her that had copied my homework we both had to endure Detention.

Anyway personally every time I had a new pair of Pumps, I always thought that they made me run faster and an article that was featured in the Telegraph Newspaper had the headline many, many years after my school days were over read: "Forget hi-tech Trainers, stick to plain Plimsolls Parents told". Children who demand the latest Nike or Adidas Trainers may be better off buying old-fashioned Plimsolls because they encourage a healthier style of running, Researchers claim, and children should be encouraged to wear shoes with thin, flexible soles such as Plimsolls from a young age to help them develop a natural 'barefoot' running style. See, I told you that they could always made me run faster!

Now I have another confession that I am sure if my Brother knew about at the time he would have bashed me for. I used to love wearing his "Monkey Boots" when he wasn't around, even though he was some considerable sizes bigger than me. Monkey Boots were really popular with kids in the 70's and could be worn by both girls and boys and were considered to be a cheap alternative to Doc Martens. Kelvin had loads of pairs of Doc Martens over the years including a pair that had about seventeen lace holes and of which used to drive me mad as he kept me waiting while he put them on and off as it used to take him a good twenty minutes to complete this task. So with Kelvin's boots firmly on my feet I would make some jam on bread, filled an old plastic squash bottle with water and stash them into my Brother's army haversack bag and take off for the day. Sometimes I would go alone or with friends over the fields for miles and miles until I reached the M6 motorway where I used to make a Den in the bushes and hedgerows that bordered the fields and just spend the day there out of the way. Other times I would get up early and a big gang of us would walk all the way to Corley Rocks which used to be known as Corley Cutting, these rocks were massive and made of sandstone and sat in the midst of the Warwickshire countryside. We used to spend all day there and had loads of fun trying to climb the rocks, make dens and tree swings and there was a massive overhanging rock that looked like the face of a witch, infact, I think they used to refer to her as "The Witch from Corley Rocks". If only they knew about the other Witch from our cul-de-sac, Ooh, my Dad would have loved that bit of crack I just had, as he always referred to Mam after they had separated as "The Animal".

It was on one of these occasions that Kelvin tried to get the better of me by building a tree house in one of the huge Oak trees just off the corn field next to our house. I was useless at climbing trees and he was jeering at me from up the tree as he watched my fruitless attempts to overcome this problem, in the end I stomped off "in the huff" only to appear ten minutes later carrying the solution to my earlier problem ... I had his metal bunk bed ladders which I smugly leant against the tree, he was no longer laughing. I didn't realise it at the time as I was so intent on overcoming the problem of getting up into the tree that I entirely forgot about how I was going to get back down ... now this is where I risked life and limb after making the decision to shimmy along a tree branch towards the rope swing that was suspended over the brook. This was not an easy manoeuvre and involved me more or less doing a Fireman's exit down the rope and lowering myself into the smelly brook, I felt sick with the fear of falling and my hands ached so much from gripping onto random objects that I just prayed would hold my weight.

Corley Services was another favourite place of mine to visit, it is close to the M6 Motorway near to our village, being about 3 miles away, I used to love jumping on my bike and taking off down all the country lanes and short cuts to get to the Service Station, you see, it had my favourite thing there ... A Bouncy Castle! Once I had paid, there was no limit to the amount of time I spent on it. It must have taken me ages to ride the 6 miles there and back on my little bike but it was worth it in my eyes so much so that I didn't very often share this pleasure with any of my friends.

Chapter 9

Knock Three Times –
(Tony Orlando & Dawn)

I mentioned earlier that Kelvin and I were bitter enemies and because he is older than me it meant that he was also stronger than me which in effect meant that I had limited resources on how to get the better of him when we fought. One way was for me to take the mickey out of him by demanding in public "Go on then spell pond" knowing full well that "bomp" "dond" etc. would be spelt out by him. Mam always said that he was Dyslexic you see but I am really not sure if this is the case or if it was one of my Mam's flippant comments. As it happens it was the Daughter of Paddy that taught my Brother to write as he was struggling to do "S and 5's" and still to this day he has an odd way of writing them. The other one I used to get him with was "Go on then tie your shoelaces" knowing full well that I could and he couldn't. Kids are so cruel and there was never any boundary to our fights infact it was nothing to pull each other's hair out by the clump or to bite or scratch one another causing various degrees of injuries. Kelvin used to really hurt and annoy me by rapping his knuckles on my head or punching me in the stomach; it didn't matter to him that Dad told him time and time again that boys don't hit girls. Even now, as an Adult, I have to admit that I am intolerant of anyone touching my head, infact, if someone were to do the same to me now then it is highly likely that I would go wild with them.

Mam and Dad used to get sick of our bickering and peace would only reign when we were either asleep or apart from each other and it was always a challenge to see who could get the better of who and as such Kelvin got one up on me most Saturday nights because Mam used to tell us that we had to be in bed by 9pm while she was out, the only problem with this was that I couldn't tell the time and he could. He always used to commandeer the television and have "Match of the Day" on which is highly suspicious to me as I am sure that it was broadcasted at 10pm! Kelvin was also responsible for spoiling my fantasy of Christmas by telling me that "Santa Claus" did not actually exist. I was devastated so much so that I cried myself to sleep for many nights following this harsh revelation, if the truth be known I never got over it as I loved the idea that someone would come and deliver me lots and lots of lovely presents regardless of whether or not I had been good. That's not all, he also terrified me by telling me that the ice on the outside of our single glazed softwood windows was infact a very bad man called "Jack Frost" who had created the ice with his breath as he was looking in at me. The sheer thought of this absolutely terrified me so much so that I used to hide myself under my bed covers and eventually fall asleep. Talking of bed covers, on rare occasions if we had to share my bed if for example Mam was decorating Kelvin's room or something similar he used to "pump" (break wind) in the bed and then hold my head under the covers so that I had to smell it ... Horrid Boy!

Every year Kelvin and Dad went to London for the day to Wembley Stadium to watch the Cup Final. I was never allowed to go as it was a boy thing! Instead I had to stay at home with

Mam and to entertain myself I would 'play out' with the rest of the Kids doing the usual stuff like riding my bike, roller skating or playing kerby. I feel the need to point out that I couldn't actually roller skate as such and it was more or less guaranteed that I would sustain an injury of some kind, mind you I have never tried ice skating either but I can boast about one thing which had four wheels and that was my skateboard, oh yes I could skateboard just fine.

One of my fondest memories was the present I used to receive from Dad and Kelvin on their return from the Final. One year I distinctly remember receiving a gift wrapped Monopoly Board game and I was thrilled to bits with it and can remember thinking that it was well worth the forfeit of going to London. Kelvin and I used to try and attempt to play Monopoly; I say attempt for a reason, his peevish behaviour always ended up with him spoiling the game to the point where you could guarantee that he would tip the board up if I reached the stage where I was beating him. He was such a Spoilsport and I used to feel so angry with him as all my money and property cards were laid out in neat little rows and his side of the board used to be in complete chaos an by the time he had tipped everything over I used to spend ages sorting the money and cards out into the correct order.

You know I mentioned my bike earlier, well; my dream bike was the Chopper which was a Wheelie Bike launched in the 1970's by Raleigh and was a "must have" item of coolness for any kid. I can't tell you how much I wanted a red one as red was my favourite colour and one Christmas morning Mam insisted on sending me and Kelvin into the Scullery to get her a glass of milk only to discover that my Brother had his dream Racer bike which was metallic blue and I had a Raleigh Commando bike. My bike was infact launched a few years after the Chopper in 1973 and was originally only available in jet black; it had a 3 speed twist-grip gear change, sissy bar, chopper seat and chrome mud/chain guards. Although at first I was downhearted I came to love my Commando just as much, infact I was gutted when much after Dad had gone, I got a puncture in my back wheel and had no one to help me to repair it and as such it just lay abandoned in the garden rusting after that never to be ridden again. There is a positive though, in September 2013 Raleigh Chopper launched their 75th Limited Edition Beano Chopper of which only 400 were made and guess who the proud owner of one is? Me!

Mam was the Boss as far as we were concerned, I say Boss but what I mean is that we were more fearful of her than we were of Dad. I can't ever remember Dad ever hitting me but that might be because I have always been a Daddy's girl and my judgement slightly biased. Mam used to "belt us" or tell us she was going to "thrape us" and the mere mention of the word 'thrape' used to scare the pants off me even though I had no idea what it meant after all a smack was a smack, wasn't it? One of the ways that Mam used to punish us was to hit us with the sole of her slipper which really hurt especially as I was so thin (Dad nicknamed me Tin Ribs) and slapping me on my bum stung basically because there was no flesh on me and I think it used to hurt Mam more than it did me because of my bony bum. If Kelvin and I "carried on" when we went to bed we used to get three warnings via Mam's slipper which she used to fling up against the living room ceiling, after the third warning we got the full Monty with her racing upstairs and sorting us out, she would be livid.

I recall getting up late one night with a blocked nose from a cold that I was suffering with at the time and making my way downstairs for a drink of water. I opened the Breakfast Room door and unbeknown to me Mam was on her hands and knees behind it painting the door. In the process of me opening the door the can of paint tipped all over the carpet, I didn't hang about and ran for my life back up to the safety of my bed with Mam in hot pursuit, she ended up following a trail of painted hand marks which were all up the banister, bedroom door and all over my blankets. I thought I would be smart and threw myself into my bed face down and used my pillow to protect my bum, this was all to no avail as she tore the bedclothes off me and almost ended up belting the life out of me. When I think back to the incident now I think Mam was extremely hard on us, infact most kids would have just got up and disturbed their Mum up but instead I was fairly self-sufficient by now and obviously just thought that I would deal with my cold myself by getting a drink of water.

I recall how house proud Mam was, she was always decorating or buying new appliances or furniture. The house always looked lovely; she had a strict cleaning regime and also had the habit of moving the furniture in each room around on a regular basis in order to change the look of each room. She took real pride in our home even down to our laundry as she even had a routine for that, all white underwear and socks were soaked in a bucket of diluted bleach then put into the laundry boiler and darks and whites were never mixed. We were fortunate enough to have the latest Twin Tub Washing Machine and she loved nothing more than pegging the sparkling whites out on the washing line in the back garden for all the neighbours to "Ooh and Aah" over. I think that it was imperative that she proved that she was perfect in all aspects of her life. Mam's cleaning routine extended to the car, shed, garden and garage with nothing daring to be out of place and it was a common occurrence to see her outside sweeping the paths and the pavement which was in front of our house.

The village has a claim to fame: The Actor Clive Owen was born in 1964; he made his film debut in "Vroom" 1987, soon after played the starring role in the TV Series "Chancer" 1990. His international popularity surged when he played DCI Ross Tanner in "Second Sight" 1999, his first major Hollywood film was "The Rich Man's Wife" 1996 and the list goes on but the film I remember him the most for was when he played the Assassin in "The Bourne Identity" 2002 alongside Matt Damon. Also the Musician Roddy 'Radiation' Byers born in 1955 who played lead guitar for Ska Band 'The Specials' and well known for playing classics such as "Concrete Jungle" and "Hey Little

Rich Girl" and writing hits such as "Rat Race". Personally, I preferred the group Madness and in particular the 1979 song "One Step Beyond" and can distinctly remember the year I went on the annual school trip to Blackpool and me and my school friends rode 'The Haunted Swing' whilst listening to 'Ghost Town' by The Specials which was an amazing song at the time.

As a family we were fortunate enough to have a number of holidays every year, one being our regular one at Wallis's Holiday Camp in Cayton Bay near to Scarborough, it just so happens that my extended family went there for 26 years in a row and my Grandma Greta's claim to fame was when Bill Maynard (Greengrass) from the television programme Heartbeat arrived at her caravan one night very drunk insisting that it was his caravan.

The history of the Camp started in the 1930's well before it was taken over by Wallis's in 1946 and the Camp jingle was "Wallidays are Jollidays". Even today I can recall the dual cycles that I loved to ride on around the campsite with my Mam and Dad upfront pedalling and me and my Brother on the bench seat behind them. There was the Pavilion which housed the Rendezvous Club that kept the Grown Ups happy all holiday and I think this is where I can recall my first accident ... On opening the caravan door from the inside I was just about to go out into the blustery weather when the unthinkable happened, the wind took the door with me still holding the handle and flung me like a rag doll up against a low white picket fence which was just a couple of feet away from the road. Mam rushed to soothe me but was helpless with laughing recalling this rather bizarre accident. I on the other hand was beside myself crying more because my pride was hurt and also because I was annoyed at seeing her behaving like that Tut! The thing is that in all honesty my Mam was not the only one who was helpless with laughter as so were some other family members Hmm. Strangely enough the 1998 film "Little Voice" which starred Brenda Blethyn, Jane Horrocks,

Michael Caine, Ewan McGregor and Jim Broadbent to name a few was filmed in Scarborough infact, the Mr Boo Nightclub scenes were filmed at Wallis's Cayton Bay Holiday Centre in The Palladium which has sadly since been demolished. After watching this film I felt that it was uncanny the resemblance Brenda Blethyn's character and our Mam had, right down to the physical appearance and her mannerisms, to put it bluntly she presented herself as nothing other than a drunken old slapper.

Holidaying in Morecombe in a touring caravan was a once only experience ... My parents hired a small four berth touring caravan and Dad experienced the complexities of towing first hand; this resulted in us finally arriving at our destination in a rather nervous state. It rained all holiday and Mam and Dad let me choose a clown puppet to entertain me. He had a green suit with white polka dots on and red boots and I had great fun playing with him in the puddles that is until Kelvin rather peevishly jumbled all his strings together and do you know what I never managed to untangle Mr Clown ...?

Another regular trip we would have was to Blackpool Illuminations. It was fantastic as we used to meet up with most of our family and stay in a Guest House that had the rule of asking all Guests to vacate their Rooms for the day once breakfast was over and even though we were out all day the time used to fly by. The illuminations or lights as we called them were amazing and I was fascinated every year as they would be a different theme. I used to enjoy the tram rides up and down the front and sometimes I would be so tired from walking that Dad used to sit me on his shoulders to give my legs a rest. Everything about this little 'Mini Break' was great including the food which was totally 'Bum Ting' especially the Fish and Chips because they were cooked in Dripping and wrapped in newspaper. Fish and Chips never tasted as good as they did on these holidays and afterwards we had Candy Floss which was utterly divine.

Some years later my Maternal Grandparents bought a six berth Bluebird Static Caravan on a small site in North Wales, Granda had by now retired from the Pit and so they were free to travel anytime and enjoy time away from home. Granda would load up his Metallic Green Hillman Hunter ready for the trip including their blue electric mower so that they could keep the tiny little garden area surrounding the Bluebird nice and tidy. The caravan had a double bedroom, bunk bed room and space to convert the table into an extra double bed, a cottage suite, coffee table and a black and white TV occupied the living room area the TV was a bit choosy about its reception and we always complained about it to Granda but he just said it was because we were so close to the Welsh Mountains which apparently interfered with the reception but I wasn't too sure. Also there was an electric fire in the living room area, it was infact the only source of heating in the caravan and when the Grown Ups went out for the evening we were warned never to put the fire on and given our history it was probably the most sensible rule to abide by.

My Brother and I used to alternate our time in the caravan once Mam and Dad had separated, if Mam wasn't going to the van with Grandma and Granda then only one of us could go at a time as our Grandparents couldn't cope with our constant bickering and fighting as by now we were 'knocking seven bells' out of each other. I think this is an old naval expression for giving someone a good thrashing. Sometimes "knocking a man for six" which is a Cricketing term could presumably lead to "knock all eight bells" out of a man would be to kill him either that or seven is a lucky number as there are seven days in the week, seven deadly sins, seven colours of the rainbow …

Anyway the electricity to the van was run off a Shilling Meter which was in the broom cupboard and the kitchen sink operated with a slop bucket underneath the van. The emptying of the slop bucket was not a particularly nice job to have to undertake, fresh water was collected from various stand pipes located around the site and the grown-ups used to keep us busy doing one or the other chore. The broom cupboard doubled as a bathroom at night with the aid of a bright orange plastic bucket which we had to wee in if we were desperate Yuk! If this was the case the sound effects from us urinating in the bucket rang out throughout the caravan and left the rest of the family in no doubt as to the purpose of our visit.

Granda made a small washing line out of two brush stales which had a 6 foot length of washing line tied to it. We could only fit a few pairs of pants, socks or tea towels on it but in fairness it did the job just fine. The kitchen sink doubled up as the place to have a wash down but Grandma was extremely strict in that she insisted we had separate bowls for our personal wash and a different bowl for the everyday kitchen items. The Site toilets and Shower Blocks were across the other side of our field and the rule was that under no circumstances were we allowed to wander over to the Blocks in the middle of the night no matter which call of nature was looming, even the showers were operated off a Shilling and Mam always insisted that I shared the shower with her which meant one thing me dithering again freezing cold waiting for Mam to finish first so that I could then get under. What is it with me and water? Behind the toilet block was a tall wooden gate which used to lead into a small housing estate, we used this as a short cut to the Beach. My Brother used to go to the beach after breakfast every morning and I was always sent to find him at lunchtime. How he spent all those hours playing skimming on the beach I don't know, in my eyes it wasn't even a nice beach as it was hell to walk on due to the huge pebbles.

Sometimes our Grandma and Granda used to get two deckchairs out of the boot of the car and sit on the beach to watch us play (obviously not together) and I will always remember seeing my Grandma with a woollen blanket covering her legs and the wind whipping up and making her headscarf thrash about her. After the beach we always used to play on the slot machines with Granda while Mam and Grandma played on the 'flip' Bingo in the Amusement Arcade, four corners won 1 token and a full line either horizontally, vertically or diagonally won 2 tokens. This was no ordinary bingo, this was serious stuff as tradition had it that all tokens were saved until the very end of the holiday. We all waited with baited breath to choose the Prize: a multi-coloured glass fish or clown ornament, plastic biscuit barrel, spare toilet roll doll, dustpan and brush ... You're getting the picture aren't you? Also overlooking the beach was a detached Café which Kelvin happened to visit some considerable years later when he was on one of his day trips and found that it was nothing more than a greasy spoon Cafe. Funny how things actually are rather than how you always thought they would be, it always looked lovely from the outside with huge windows overlooking the beach and red canopies adorning the windows.

These holidays in our Grandparents caravan were something that we not only did when Dad had gone but we did when he was still with us, infact all the family used the van at some point during the year but once Dad had left we used to squash in Grandma and Granda's car with Mam and go away for a week with the highlight of the holiday being a day trip to Rhyl where we used to visit the big Outdoor Market, walk along the Seafront and if we were lucky ride the Funfair. I always loved to see the 'Horror Crypt' which had a 1:1 scale King Kong on the top (head, shoulders and two forearms with fists clasping bent iron rods, presumably from a cage breakout). Under King Kong there were four glass windows that gave you an example of what to expect inside, one window showed a rotating hanged-man with tongue and eyes bulging out and another displayed three heads on spikes with blood pouring out from underneath them. On one of these trips Mam started bidding at the fresh fish stall and won nine Plaice for 45 pence, which she later cooked in the oven in milk and butter, such a strange thing for me to recall, funny thing was that I just thought that the fish were a waste of time as they were full of bones and I have never been a lover of Plaice since.

During one particular trip I came up with the hair brained idea of buying an airbed and trying to surf on it. All my holiday spends were used up in one go so that I could purchase a bright red one and I couldn't wait to try it out so after going to the shop next to the Bird's Eye shop I headed straight to the beach where I promptly inflated the airbed and headed for the waves. I had such high hopes and was bursting with excitement as I put the airbed onto the surface of the water, I carefully placed one foot on top and tried to put my other foot on all the while trying to maintain an upright stance ready to surf … the airbed sank to the seabed and I was up to my knees in freezing cold water. I just didn't understand what had gone wrong with my theory … what a waste of time, another dream shattered.

I also distinctly remember that on the 16th August 1977 we were on holiday at the caravan, infact, we were in the 'Family Room' of a local pub when we heard that Elvis Aaron Presley "The King of Rock 'n' Roll" had been found dead at the age of 42 years. It was reported that "The King" was found in the bathroom of his Graceland home after he had been on the toilet. He had then fallen off onto the floor and was found by his Fiancée Ginger Alden lying in a pool of his own vomit. All attempts to save him failed and he was pronounced dead at 7pm. It transpired that several years of drug abuse had severely deteriorated his health and the cause of death was supposedly a cocktail of ten prescribed drugs, taken in doses that no Doctor would prescribe. The Nation went into mourning waiting patiently for any scrap of news to filter over from America, even I felt sad as I thought he was extremely handsome, had a great voice and was an amazing dancer and it all felt such a shame and total waste of a very talented person plus dying on the toilet in my eyes was certainly no way to die.

It was during one of these trips with Grandma and Granda that we could no longer ignore Mam's strange behaviour, I felt so ashamed of her the morning after one her nights out and didn't even want to be in her company. You see she had gone out for the evening with Grandma and Granda to the local Club which was on the seafront. Some hours later my Grandparents returned to the caravan without her and I could sense some anxiety or maybe it was disapproval from my Grandma but couldn't work out what the problem was and after having some supper Kelvin and I went to bed. It was a warm night so we had the bunk bed windows open on the small lever catches which roughly tilted the windows out by about two inches, sometime later we were woken suddenly by a commotion outside our caravan. We soon recognised the voice of our very drunk Mam who had been escorted back to the caravan by a very drunk strange man. Anyway things got out of hand as the goodnight kiss progressed to a full performance with sound effects of them having sex up against the old Bluebird no less than six feet away from our little bedroom and more or less on the main caravan door and it is since that day that I have always tried to hide my shame by saying that it was a case of "wax on" "wax off" on the side of the caravan. This was just the start of things to come ...

Chapter 10

Tonsils to ...

I'm not sure if I mentioned to you that Dad was never a Gardener or into 'Do it yourself' but one day he eagerly took delivery of a brand new petrol Suffolk Punch lawn mower. It was massive and made short work of our very large triangular shaped back garden, we didn't have borders to maintain or anything fancy but he kept the grass nice for us to play on, to be honest, he couldn't tell a flower or weed apart. Once the garden was looking in good shape he decided to take on two rather ambitious projects, one being the digging of a very deep garden pond and the other converting the garden shed into a Pigeon Cree. The first project got off to a flying start with a very large, deep hole being dug by hand, lined and then filled and stocked with goldfish and plants and was finished off with a beautiful rockery that he had designed to surround it. Once the pond was complete the following morning much to Dad's horror he discovered that the pond had almost totally drained, further investigation revealed that the pond liner had a hole in it but thankfully you will be pleased to know that he did manage to rescue the situation with the aid of a hosepipe and without any fatalities. The other project also going reasonably well with Dad recycling an old internal door which I think was taken off the doorway in between the Scullery and the Breakfast Room, he used this as the base of the pigeon loft which was raised about three or four feet from the shed floor, I say quite well because there seemed to be only one size nail that Dad was using for the project and they were 6 inch ones and he managed to convert the shed using only two tools, a hand saw and a hammer. If I was to be honest I think he did a really good job and at least he kept it nice and clean for his Pigeons. Our front garden was lower than the level of the street pavement and we used to share access to the property with our Welsh Neighbours. The garden at the front, although small, was quite impressive as it was built in a terraced style and was decorated with large rockery stones. Arabis (Rock Cress) which has small white four-petalled flowers and Aubretia plants cascaded over the edges of the terraces and made the front smell sweet and look very pretty. Sometimes if we had heavy rain the drains would be unable to cope and with our house being the last one in the cul-de-sac plus it also being right next to the open fields it meant that all the rain water from the field would engulf the property, swallowing up our gardens and anything else that crossed its path. This was great for us kids as it meant that we could play out in our wellies, but not the orange ones! Luckily for us the aftermath of a storm would be to the outside of our house only, much to Mam and Dad's relief but Mam was never amused as the drains also used to burst along with the sewers which meant one thing ... what went down the loo soon came back to the surface!

This brings me to the other topic of Dad and his hobbies ... Homing pigeons! Hours and hours I would stand in the garden with my Dad shaking a plastic tub that he kept the corn in repeatedly shouting out in the direction of the sky "Come on, come on" Susie, Susan, Sukie etc. (I think he loved the name Susan) and of course we would still be standing there to this day if he hadn't given up on buying homing pigeons Tut! I even came home from school one day to discover that my Tortoise and Rabbit had both been swapped without my consent for some more homing pigeons! Jeez, nothing was safe from Dad and his good old fashioned bartering! Oh and then there was the time that my Dad went out with his Air Rifle and shot a Pigeon which he insisted that we cook and eat. He brought it home and had to ask a lady called Julie to pluck it and gut it Eerh! Mam flatly refused to eat it and soon showed her distaste when Dad said that we would eat it and to be honest it was nice apart from when we came across the lead pellet that was still in the bird after it had been roasted. Julie cut the talons off and I spent the rest of the week chasing my friends around the school playground whilst manually operating its claw like foot via its tendons which were left exposed so I was able to make the foot do a claw like grip much to my friend's horror.

Dad's Air Rifle used to be the subject of many visits to our house by the Police, you see Dad would be reading the Newspaper, gardening or watching the TV with us when there would be a knock at the front door and when he answered the door two Police Officers would be standing on the doorstep and would ask Dad if everything was ok? "Yes no problem Officers, what can I help you with"? We've had a report from your Wife that you've been threatening to shoot her with a gun! What the hell? He'd done no such thing but Mam used to get what she wanted as Dads gun would be confiscated leaving him bewildered as to what the problem was as they hadn't even had an argument, that's how twisted she is though.

Auntie May and Uncle Joe were by now married and had a bought a new four bedroomed house in Chatsworth Drive which was nearby and on the other side of the Pool and Park. Their wedding was another area for disaster for me as I think Mam had boldered on in there and just assumed that I would be Auntie May and Uncle Joe's Bridesmaid even though I'm not sure if that was what either of them wanted, either way the night before the Big Day I was sent to bed with my hair in the most enormous rollers you have ever seen. I woke the next morning with a really stiff neck due to the fact that these rollers must have made my head hover about 3 inches higher than my neck on the pillow. Just to make matters worse I was then trussed up into a lilac and white long fancy cotton dress and made to put on the most ridiculous looking gold sparkly shoes ever, I looked the biggest numpty going. The dress by the way became a 'nightie' a few months later, I have no idea what my Mam was thinking at the time but I had to wear it to bed all the same.

The Wedding Reception afterwards was held at The Nelson Pub and Auntie May and Uncle Joe had hired the upstairs room for yet another dreaded family bash, all was going well until I discovered what I thought was a rip in the back of my dress just leading up from centre of the hem. I was terrified as I knew Mam was going to 'belt me' for spoiling this very special dress, there was only one thing for it and that was for me to stand with my back against the wall on the Landing area of the stairs of the pub for the majority of the celebration daring not to move in case someone noticed the rip. All in all I must have stood there for at least 4 hours to the point where I distinctly recall my Uncle Jack trying to coax me back into the big room with him. It was only later when we returned home and I undressed that I discovered on closer inspection that the dress wasn't actually ripped but a part of the design that would allow my legs to move more freely within the dress ... Bloody Hell!

The Nelson by the way was named after one of our Greatest Heroes Lord Haratio Nelson who was a British Admiral whose Naval Career ended at Trafalgar in 1805. He can't have been much to look at in my opinion as he was blind in one eye, had no teeth and only one arm and if I am to be honest I can't actually see what his Mistress Lady Emma Hamilton saw in him. Sadly the pub was demolished in 2009 which I feel is a shame as it was built in 1806 and was an important historical pub during its lifetime. It appears to me that we have lost too many of these beautiful historical buildings.

I will never forget the time when my Brother was admitted into hospital to have his Tonsils removed. He was 11 years old at the time and I have to say that I actually felt really sorry for him post op after I saw him sitting on the toilet in the Hospital with the door open and he was crying with pain. Mam and Dad both tried to console him all to no avail. Kelvin distinctly remembers the time as it was the heatwave of 1976 and he said that the weather was so intense to the point of almost being unbearable.

The thing is I didn't get what was happening as there was a bribe of jelly and ice cream if Kelvin did a poo? Like I said I didn't get it, as what the hell had that got to do with my Brother having his Tonsils out? Some years later I think I was talking about Hospital blunders and my Brother's operation came into the conversation and how bizarre it was when Kelvin interrupted the conversation and said "Karina, I didn't really have my Tonsils out, it was my Testicle that hadn't descended" ... Oops! I wish he had told me this sooner; it would have saved me from terrifying half of my class mates with the tale of woe regarding Tonsils and toilets. As it happens he shouldn't have felt embarrassed as undescended Testicles are a common childhood condition where a boy is born without both Testicles in his Scrotum (Unilateral and Bilateral Cryptorchidism). One in twenty five boys are born without undescended Testicles and usually the Testicle(s) will move down naturally during the first three to six months of life. Anyway, Brother, the surgery that I suspect you underwent was called Orchidopery and I can't apologise enough for embarrassing you, at least no one else knows about this Hey!

During Kelvin's stay in the Hospital Mam decided to take us along to the Infant's Ward which was attached to the Children's Ward that Kelvin was on, here she introduced us to a little 2 year old girl called Trudy whom we visited on loads of occasions. Trudy's hair colour was similar to the colour of golden bales of straw that we often saw in the fields next to our house and she had the deepest of blue eyes you could ever imagine.

Everytime we went into her little room she used to be standing up at the cot side clinging onto the rail for attention, she had the smile that could melt the heart of the Devil. One day Mam dropped into the conversation that Trudy was coming to live with us and we were going to adopt her as no one else loved or wanted her. We thought that this was an amazing idea and that things were starting to look up for us as a family but one thing still bothered me, what had come over Mam? She was being extra nice and kind. Anyway, Kelvin and I started referring to Trudy as our new little Sister and spent hours chatting to her about all sorts of things, I think we both felt sorry for her because she was confined to the cot, she was cute beyond words, infact almost doll like. Unfortunately, our chance of a new family life soon came crashing down as the adoption didn't go ahead for reasons I honestly don't know which was a real shame as by now we had made a bond with this little girl and it tore me up inside as she went out of our lives as quickly as she had entered them. Had Mam done this on purpose? It felt to me like we had lost Charlie all over again!

Now my close shave with the hospital was when I was at the Park with my friends and I was overcome with the most overwhelming pain in my back, it became unbearable and I think I must have collapsed. One of my Friend's must have had the common sense to go and fetch my Mam as she suddenly appeared at the Park in the white car. She gently carried me in her arms back to the car all the while talking to me and reassuring me. This was my Mam, the Mam I loved so much and she was back just the way I remember her when we used to watch the television together and 'Watch with Mother' used to be on. Mam gently lay me down on the back seat of the car and drove immediately to the Village Surgery, once inside she lay me down on the wooden type pew like benches in the Waiting Room and before I knew it Dr Cooper diagnosed Pleurisy, which is the inflammation of the Pleura, the lining surrounding the lungs. You know I have to say that I have never felt pain like it. Mam and Dad nursed me at home where I stayed on the settee as it was too painful for me to be moved around. Dad used to carry me to the toilet and Mam waited on me hand, finger and thumb. Dr Cooper came in daily but unfortunately after about two weeks I was still losing weight due to my lack of appetite so he gave me an ultimatum, either I started to eat and gain some weight or it was the Hospital for me. Mam came to my rescue and saved the day because she managed to tempt me into eating these little individual trifles that you could buy and slowly but surely I began to feel better and start to put a little weight back on which in turn saved me from the dreaded Hospital.

Dad's close shave with the Hospital pardon the pun was when he had a Vasectomy, apparently my Parents had decided (not sure if it was both that made the decision) that our little family was complete therefore Dad would have the 'Snip'! All was going well following the procedure until he discovered that Mam was still taking the Contraceptive Pill Oops! I seem to recall that he found Mams secret stash of her pill under a loose floorboard or somewhere similar in their bedroom, anyway there was hell on in our house as well you can imagine as it only confirmed to our Dad that his suspicions were true and Mam had been doing the dirty on him. Following this Mam dealt a final blow to Dad and spat the following words out at him "One of the Bairns is yours and one isn't". Jeez she really was stooping low and if you could see us with our Dad you would have no doubt whatsoever in your mind that he had fathered both of us. My Brother and I feel extremely lucky to have our Dad as I am glad to say that he never ever had any doubt in his mind that we weren't his Children.

I will never forget the day that Dad left Mam for the final time, it was quite pleasant weather wise and I was playing outside in the cul-de-sac just outside our house with some friends when Dad appeared from the house carrying our brown leather suitcase, now on reflection I cannot pinpoint anything specific happening in our household, there wasn't any argument or fight that stands out to me but obviously something had happened. I ran to him and he picked me up, we hugged and gave each other one of our pursed lips kisses and once he had lowered me back down I ran back to my friends and carried on playing. I wasn't alarmed or frightened and can only put this down to the fact that maybe because I had witnessed this situation before it didn't really sink in what was going on or maybe it was because of the way Dad handled the situation in that he didn't want to discuss what was happening for fear of leaving me in a distressed state either way it must have been dreadful beyond words for him to leave us. My Brother thinks that the events of this particular day must have been the turning point for our Dad as he fought the Courts for years to gain Custody of me and my Brother, all unfortunately to no avail. The battle was ongoing between him and Mam for many years to come, unfortunately back in the 70's it was practically unheard of for the Father to be awarded Sole Custody of the children and taken from their Mother, had that not been the case our lives would have been very different I am sure, either way it is what it is and nothing in the world can change the past. Last year when Auntie Marjorie and I were chatting she told me that at the time Dad had secured a Colliery house for us shortly after he had moved back for the final time to the North-East. She said that he had collected the keys to the property so that they could determine what work needed to be undertaken and completed in preparation for our arrival. After the house viewing was complete they both agreed that it needed a good clean and total decoration throughout but apart from that it would have been ideal for us as we would have been really close to our family thus Dad having the support that he so desperately needed for all of us. Auntie Marjorie said that things were going really well until the great big 'Cloud of Doom' arrived and Dad was devastated to discover that another Miner at the Pit where he was working threw a 'Spanner in the Works' as he kicked up such a fuss demanding to know why a Single man was being allocated a Colliery house and that my friend is basically where the story ends as Dad had to reluctantly return the keys back to the Pit and face up to the truth that we were never going to live together again.

It was after Dad had returned to the North-East that it became apparent to the rest of his Siblings what state of mind he was in as he had lost so much weight, his body shook uncontrollably and he had started to stutter a little when he spoke. What the hell had my Mam done to my Dad? Thankfully the family soon turned him around with a little tender loving care and patience and he eventually started to get back to being his old self. Although Dad was beginning to look better physically as he had put a little bit of weight back on and was sleeping much better he still had to face the turmoil of attending the Court Hearings which were being held in Warwickshire. He travelled countless times to be present at each Hearing and was bitterly disappointed as some of the Hearings would have to be rescheduled for a later date because Mam didn't even bother to turn up to them claiming to be ill. I overheard her many a time asking Dr Cooper for a note to excuse her from Court which in my opinion only made the situation regarding the battle of our Custody linger on far longer than it should have done.

It was while Dad was on these journeys that Mam used to 'play up'. He used to stay at a former Colleagues house and she used to get drunk and get in such an intoxicated state it was unreal, she thought nothing of going to Dads Colleagues house and pleading with him to have her back, make a go of things again, thankfully he no longer fell for that. I must admit that I laughed my socks off when she went to Dad's Colleagues house one particular night, she was in such a drunken stupor that she must have 'lost all leave of her senses' as she beseeched Dad through the letterbox only to have the door opened by the man of the house only to be told that she had got her dates mixed up and Dad wasn't due to arrive until the day after. She also used to involve me by sending me up to the very same house to ask for my Dad. I think that she was trying everything by now to get him back even to the point of writing my Dad letters saying that Kelvin would end up in Borstal. I've got these letters, a whole shoebox full of them which Dad had saved for me until I became an adult, God they are good, infact she is a unique human being as according to the letters she has had seven Hysterectomies'! Funny thing is that my Solicitor read these letters and during my next appointment she said that they were brilliant to read, infact, she had taken them home and opened a bottle of wine and had the most entertaining evening she had had in a while. Having said that, I think the main thing to point out here is that life was all about Mam and as such we had no choice but to follow her, falling into place along the way with whatever decisions she made. She was selfish and ruthless beyond words and on reflection I think that she eventually reached the point where our family were never surprised at her antics. I think her overall aim at this time was to get Dad to feel sorry for her and there was never any limit to how far she would stoop to get what she wanted even to the point of trying to take her own life. I am now convinced that these attempts were never serious but as a Child I initially thought that each attempt she made was serious as I would often find her in a collapsed state having taken an overdose of Valium (Diazepam) along with other medication. Diazepam affects chemicals in the brain that may become unbalanced and cause anxiety and is also used to treat anxiety disorders, alcohol withdrawal symptoms (I wish!) or muscle spasms. It was times like these that I would run to find my Brother and with each of us on either side of her we were able to prop her up and try and walk her around the living room all the while with her vomiting into a bucket, we also used to try and talk to her in the hope that she wouldn't lose consciousness until an Ambulance arrived to take over. I think it was about this time that I began to sense Kelvin's intolerance towards our Mam, I felt completely helpless to deal with her on my own and prayed that he could hang on in there for me and I have to say he did his best to try and support me but I think he reached the point of "pressing the self-preservation button", you see, he was just a kid too and it's important that you remember that as he was also in turmoil trying to understand what was going on, what did he need to do? Afterall he had become the 'Man of the House' hadn't he and he would have wanted to show our Dad that he was doing his best for us. Should we have witnessed any of these situations or dramas? No, but sadly for us it was a weekly occurrence, where were the authorities I hear you ask yourself? All I can remember is that we had a Social Worker called Phil who used to come to the house now and again, anything beyond that I cannot tell you, as far as I can see though because we had food in the cupboards, a clean home to live in and good school attendance, I don't think that they saw us as being 'At Risk'. How many times have I wanted to go into Care? I can't tell you, anything would have been better than the life we were living and the only consolation for me was that my Dad was not being tortured everyday too. After all what was the point of all three of us being subjected to the abuse week in week out? Even so something was really odd about this whole situation as we never really discussed any events with Dad and I don't know if that was to protect him or if it was also to protect our Mam as we obviously knew by now that some of the things that were happening to us were just not right, maybe just maybe, we knew that Mam would get into trouble. Either way I suspect that he knew partial bits of what was going on as he knew our Mam better than anyone else in the whole world, also Dad stayed in touch with some of his Colleagues from the Pit who no doubt told him what was going on when he was on one of his visits and as such I am sure that it must have been extremely painful for him to hear some of the antics that Mam got up to, as for us, I think we just felt hopeless and anything we said would be pointless and would only worry Dad even more than he already was. It wasn't like our Dad wouldn't listen to us because he would but it was just too painful to relive and spending time away from Mam with our Dad was our only respite and a time to cherish and savour and I think it is only fair to say that the reality was that both of our Parents lived in completely different worlds. Hmm it pains me to say that even though both of my Parents had come from good families it didn't seem to make any difference to my Mam how much she embarrassed herself or us.

I always thought that I was 9 when Mam and Dad finally separated but Dad said that I was 10, either way I had a rebellious streak running through me by now and as such I decided to stage my own little war on the village by sneaking around the nearby streets one night and unscrewing seventeen chrome wing mirrors off the neighbour's cars and stashing the evidence in the house. A few days later I noticed one of the round mirrors hanging by a piece of wool in our bathroom and Mam was standing in front of it doing her make-up, not sure if I ever told you about her make-up routine? You see she used to drink Gold Label Barley Wines when she was getting ready to go out for the evening. I counted seven bottles one night which were neatly lined up on the top of the toilet cistern, which only meant one thing; she was already three sheets to the wind before she had even left the house. Mam always played music during this preparation time and by the time she was ready to go out she would be slurring her words, she was just so embarrassing but the funny thing to me was that it was almost like she was revving herself up ready to go out and have a hell of a night out in the process, had the drink masked some insecurity in her? I don't think so but I guess that it could have been a possibility and at this stage in my life I am trying so hard to find reasons for my mam's bizarre behaviour. Mam's physical appearance had begun to change too, she had put weight on, probably down to all the alcohol she was drinking, plus she started to apply her make-up differently and I personally thought it was getting more and more bizarre to the point where she was putting her mascara and eye shadow on and she was looking more and more like Elizabeth Taylor when she played the part of Cleopatra in the 1963 film. With Dad gone this meant that the road was clear for Mam to legitimately 'Play the Field' so to speak and as such she had a series of Boyfriends who strangely enough nearly all had a Trade or Skill and in no particular order the following men were introduced to us; Fraser who at the time reminded me of Bjorn Ulvaeus from the pop group Abba, he was the local Plumber and drove a navy blue Morris Minor van, I remember him having a little blonde haired boy who I think was called Oscar, he was ok and didn't cause us any problems as such but Dad said that he thinks that it was the excitement of Mam's affair with him that finally put the last nail in her coffin regarding their marriage. One day Kelvin remembers going downstairs into the Breakfast Room where he noticed blood near to the fire, he said that Dad had found out about Mams affair with Fraser and had punched him; this is when he knew that the marriage was finally over and he had no other choice but to accept it. Not long afterwards their affair 'went public' and caused rumblings in our village as the tongues began to wag as the Villagers were saying that Mam and Fraser were having sex in the back of his work van. I have no doubt that this was infact true as I distinctly remember the whispering and nudging going on when I was out with Mam at the local Shops.

I mentioned Pete earlier who was a Mechanic and as it turned out was quite a sensible chap who I quite liked, God only knows what he was doing with my Mam. Ray who pretended to be a Policeman for God only knows what reason, I'll tell you about him a bit later and Dom who I had no idea of his profession and last but by no means least Elliott who was a Painter and Decorator who I absolutely detested him for reasons I shall tell you about later ... The first time I met him he was wearing a Pin striped suit, Bowler hat, Chelsea style black leather boots and was carrying a large black umbrella and gave the impression of looking like a swanky City Banker with him being all suited and booted. He had a distinct thick, red scar running down from his eye into his cheek which looked like it had been caused by a knife; he also had a beard and a moustache in the style of a goatee. I seem to recall that there was some suggestion that he had just been released from Prison and my first impression was that he was a Bad Man, something that he very much proved to be, maybe his attire was following his release from Prison or maybe he wore it for a Court Appearance either way it is something that I will never really know the truth about.

Now even though my Parents marriage was over my Dad truly loved and respected his in-laws even though he found it difficult with my Grandma at times. He said that Granda was an Angel sent from Heaven and that he had never met a man quite like my Granda before. The difficulty Dad faced with regard to Grandma was that Mam used to write letters to them or she would telephone them when they were at the Club on a Friday or Saturday night, you see they didn't have a telephone at home in those days and neither did we so any conversations had to be conducted over the telephone from the Public Telephone Box in the village to the tiny Telephone Kiosk at the Club which used to be awkward for Grandma to get to because of her disability. Following these telephone calls Mam would upset my Grandparents by telling them that Dad had done all sorts to her. He didn't blame my Grandma for her reaction to him after all she was only doing what any Parent would do and that was to come down on the side of their child. Ooh, before we go on I should tell you that Mam's letter writing still goes on to this day even at the age of 69 years, she is relentless and must feel great satisfaction writing to all of her family with the most twisted, spiteful and malicious things you could ever imagine. I just don't understand why she thinks she has the right to judge other people and therefore have no idea why she feels the need to repeatedly do this to her own flesh and blood, another question unanswered I fear …

During my Parents years together or apart, Dad always made time to visit my Grandparents even if the reception was a little frosty at times. He persevered though and when I was about 14 years old he turned the corner with my Grandma as she told me that she was sorry if she had badly judged my Dad and that she knew that it was Mam and her bad behaviour that was to blame for their problems. I can't tell you the relief my Dad felt after Grandma made her peace with him, he felt so much better because he had maintained throughout that it wasn't just him to blame, he after all was realistic to acknowledge that he wasn't entirely blameless in the downfall of their relationship but he didn't want my Grandparents to hate him for something that he hadn't done.

My Mam's Brother Jack came to visit us and decided to stay with us for a few days; I think he was having marital problems with his Wife Carol with whom he had three children Denise, Daniel and Mark. After a few days Uncle Jack told Mam that he was planning on returning home and Mam thought it would be a good opportunity to hitch a ride back with him, so with the travel plans in place and our Cat Kitty sitting in-between my Brother and me on the journey we set off to go back to Staffordshire ready to catch up with the family. All was going well with the journey with Mam in the front and Kelvin and I sat in the back and Kitty settled in her basket in between us until someone noticed a distinct smell of … Shit! Oh my God, it was overwhelming and my Uncle Jack had no choice but to swiftly makes plans to manoeuvre the car over to the hard shoulder of the M6 Motorway where he proceeded to frantically shout repeatedly back at us "Throw it out", "Throw it out" and that was where the problems started because Kelvin threw the Cat out onto the motorway and not the basket. The whole drama left me somewhat dazed in the back of the car, I was also trying to contain the contents of my stomach as I realised that a rather large poo which was similar in shape to a Gorilla's finger and stunk to high heaven was still in the basket right next to me. Seconds passed but it felt like minutes until both Kelvin and I sprang into action and focussed our attention on trying to coax Kitty from the motorway embankment back into the car. A whole fifteen minutes passed during which time my nerves were shot to bits as my mind was jumping around from one bad thought to the next all the while the traffic continued to hurtle past us and I was terrified that a disaster would follow if Kitty dared to venture onto the carriageway which thankfully she didn't, that cat must have been really stupid to get back in the car with us and must definitely have used one of its nine lives that particular day.

It was during this time that my Mam's relationship turned somewhat sour with my Uncle Jack, you see it was while he was on this particular visit and they had gone to the Club for a night out that it all went pear shaped, apparently, it was while Uncle Jack was standing at the Bar waiting to be served that he heard a bloke say to another bloke "God who is she going with now"? Can you imagine the anger that he must have felt? Someone saying derogative comments about his Sister, to top it all Mam was none the wiser at this point but it soon became fairly obvious afterwards that things between Brother and Sister would never be the same and that is how the situation remains with them to this very day infact I think it is fair to say that my Uncle Jack on the rare occasions that he sees Mam he 'tolerates' her.

Kitty's next unfortunate incident was when Mam had made a strawberry jelly and put it into the fridge to set. When Mam was ok we always had jelly, tinned fruit and evaporated cream early evening on a Sunday usually following pink salmon sandwiches. I was colouring at the table and Mam was busying herself and I remember going to the fridge to get a glass of milk, about five minutes later I went back to the fridge to see if the jelly had set and guess who I found inside the fridge ... Kitty swimming around in the jelly bowl completely covered, how that cat didn't suffocate I'll never know but by now I had a rather distressed red cat that couldn't wait to get out of there, poor thing must have sneaked in when I went to get my drink of milk, either way she had the huff on with me for quite a few days afterwards. This was not the end of Kitty's adventures or surprises either as one day ... Pete the Boyfriend who I mentioned earlier had a rare, bottle green, two door Alfa Romeo which he parked on our drive, I am led to believe that there were only seven of these cars imported into the UK at the time and they were originally white. I decided to take some time out and go and sit in this car as it was beautifully comfy with thick black leather seats the size of armchairs, only when I got into it did I realise I was not alone ... Turning to face my fear I discovered Kitty in the rear foot well with a beautiful litter of tortoiseshell and black and white Kittens, on closer inspection it was fairly obvious to me that she had recently given birth to them as she was still on the cleaning up process following the birth. I was chuffed to bits and played Nurse to them all fetching and carrying everything that Kitty needed including extra food and milk to help to keep her strong. I even had the foresight to leave the Drivers window down slightly so that she could come and go as she pleased, she was a good Mum and I had great fun cuddling each of the four Kittens and I am glad to say that Mam found good homes for all of them. Pete in my opinion was the only nice Boyfriend Mam had, he never gave us any cause to worry, and I only wish that he had stayed.

Chapter 11

Happy Together – (The Turtles)

At some point Dad met Vera (Wife No.2) and after a very short Courtship of about three months they were married. A marriage, may I add, that barely lasted twelve months due to her deceitful nature. They lived in a three bedroomed house in a small village just around the corner from my Uncle Bobby. I cannot ever recall being told about the plans for the wedding and only found out after the deed was done and Dad became Step-Father to her two Children Kacie and Dane who were both younger than us. We hated going to stay with Vera as she wasn't very nice to us at all, Kelvin would have to sleep with Dane and I would have to sleep with Kacie. There was one problem with this for me and it was a bloody big one and that was down to the fact that Kacie still wet the bed, which meant that I was woken suddenly every single night after she had wet the bed, this resulted in me lying in something similar to a warm paddling pool Yuk! At this stage I would even go as far to say that I would have preferred to have topped and tailed with Kelvin to the point where I was even prepared to put up with his pumps as anything would have been better than that.

I mentioned earlier that Vera didn't like us and made no secret of this and when Dad was at work, oh yes, I forgot to mention that he wasn't allowed to take time off with us when we visited, something that had never happened before or after his relationship with Vera. She treated her own children much nicer than she did us. I didn't blame her kids after all it wasn't their fault that their Mam was horrid to us, all the same this behaviour of hers left me feeling baffled as I hadn't done anything to upset her so I guess it was just the way she felt about Dad and what she must have classed as his baggage from his previous life. It's strange really as I wouldn't have thought that my Dad was horrible to her children so I couldn't understand what her issue was with us? Every single day we had the same to eat; Peanut Butter sandwiches for lunch and Minced Beef and Onion with Dumplings for tea. When we weren't visiting she would write letters to us using red ink and would always start the letter "Dear K&K" you will not be having your usual treats for Christmas this year as your Daddy has two other children now etc. etc., do not write back to him when he asks you what you would like for your Birthdays as you will not be getting them as he has a new life here … Bloody Hell! If you're reading this Vera, you must know who you are and I would just like to say shame on you! No wonder Dad left you as you were totally unfair to him. We all know that my Dad without question handed all his wages over to you, he gave up his one social night of the week where he used to go out to the Club or Pub so that he could give you and your children a better home life and what did you do in return? You failed to pay the Household Bills choosing instead to run up debts here, there and everywhere and all this could have been avoided if only you had worked hard at the marriage and been honest with Dad you could have got through anything together, of that I am sure.

Dads second marriage had quite a significant impact on me and my thought process as I found it so hard to believe that Mam and Dad would truly never be together ever again, don't get me wrong as I mentioned earlier I was glad that they had separated but nonetheless it was still hard to believe that the ending was finally here and this thought made me feel very sad indeed as it put an end to my fairy-tale ending so to speak plus by now I was beginning to have serious doubts about my Dads taste in women as he hadn't exactly got a good track record from what I could see, having said that I have to admit that our Mam and Dad had been perfect for one another way back in the early days before all the difficulties between them began.

After Dad's marriage to Vera failed he soon got a place of his own, he didn't want to go back to my Uncle Bobby's as it was just around the corner from Vera and this probably wouldn't have helped the situation so instead my Auntie Marjorie heard of a Flat going for rent in South Market Street in the village that Dad was born in. After speaking with the Landlord her hopes were dashed as he told her that he would only rent the place out to a Single Woman, my Auntie Marjorie said that she more or less had to get on her hands and knees and beg him to rent it to Dad which of course he did in the end.

Kelvin and I went on our usual visit to see Dad with both of us really looking forward to staying in the new place as I think it was the first place that Dad had ever lived alone in and his new place happened to be a terraced house that had been divided perfectly in two, both having an upstairs and downstairs. In order to gain entry to his flat which was the property at the back of the building we had to go down an Entry Way at the front of the property passing by Davina's flat who occupied the front of the property, she was nice and always had a bit of chat with us. Dad's place was great and had a Kitchen which in itself was fine but I thought it was strange as it also had a shower cubicle in there, from here the living room led up to a set of stairs and the two bedrooms. Hmm, now where was the toilet? Oh my God you wouldn't believe it if I told you that it was outside in the yard! Can you believe that there were some properties that still had outside Netties in the 80's! Anyway the toilet may have been outside but my Dad's Sister Marjorie had done it out lovely to the point of it being palatial, so much so that Davina abandoned using her loo and took to using Dad's. The interior brick work had been white washed and the door had been glossed, air fresheners were hanging in there and it had a good supply of bleach etc. to keep it in pristine order, if it had been entered into "Best Loo" it would have won hands down, you see that was the thing with my Auntie's they were damn good at looking after Dad and setting him up with whatever he needed, one Auntie used to clean for him, another did his washing and ironing, another cooked his tea etc. etc. Spoilt boy! When we arrived for a holiday Dad's Sisters always made sure that we had lovely food in so that Dad could cook us really nice meals. One of his masterpieces was Rabbit Stew which was simply delicious or Bacon Hotpot. We loved visiting all of our Relatives as they were genuinely interested in us and we used to spend hours talking about all sorts of things apart from our home life which felt like a taboo subject to us and something that both Kelvin and I didn't want to talk about. There was one relative I didn't like visiting though and that was Dads Brother Jesse who reminded me of the character John Christie in the 1971 British Crime drama film 10, Rillington Place, which is where Richard Attenborough plays the part of Christie but John Hurt also stars in the film which tells the story of British Serial Killer Christie who commits many of his crimes in his terraced house in London. My Uncle Jesse reminded me so much of Christie it was uncanny. He was a Single Bloke at the time that lived alone and I seem to recall that there had been some kind of family argument which had turned the family upside down but all the same we used to 'do our bit' and visit him. He appeared to me to be quite religious and Kelvin and I both received 'The New Testament' and a gold leaved book called 'In his Steps' and 'One of the Two' which was written by Charles Monroe Sheldon and first published in 1897, apparently 'In his Steps' has sold more than 30,000,000 copies and ranks as one of the bestselling books of all time, of course at the time I didn't realise this. Uncle Jesse made sure that he always wrote a religious quote in each book with a traditional ink fountain pen and when I received my eighth birthday present in the post from him it was this ... 'Woodland & Hill Birds' which I loved and still have to this day. He wrote the following in it "To Karina on your birthday 3.8.75". Love from Uncle Jesse xxx "To see into another's heart, your own must first be clear". In 1978 I received the 'In his Steps' book which contained the following handwritten quote from my Uncle: "At whatever the cost we must labour on mercifully in the service of Christ". "To Karina and Kelvin in a visitation to the Parish of Lyons, Oct 13th 1978". Things changed though when I was about 14 years old and Kelvin and I had been summoned over for our annual visit, Uncle Jesse had gone to the Bank and ordered his Trunk full of Georgian Silverware to be taken out for the day. We dutifully attended and went through the usual "Umming and Arring" whilst supposedly admiring all his silver which he had displayed neatly on the dining table on top of a navy blue velvet tablecloth, this was something that we had done, year in, year out, for as long as I can remember and if I was to be honest it really wasn't something I was interested in at that age. Uncle Jesse then said to me "Karina if you keep visiting me, I shall leave you everything in my will" well that comment hit me like a bolt of lightning from the sky as it felt like he was going to control me too and as far as I could see I felt that I was done with my Uncle, from then on I never went back to see him until much later in life and then only about twice, both times under duress may I add.

Dad's Girlfriend by now was a woman called Linda who was really nice and great company to be around, I think she was only about 28 years old at the time and was therefore about ten years younger than Dad. I got the impression that it wasn't serious between them and was more of a case of them just enjoying each other's company because I got the distinct impression that my Dad was a little bit lonely, she was nice to us and we got on well with her much to our relief. One evening we had all gone back to Dad's flat with a Chinese take-away,

Dad's favourite Chinese meal by the way was Chicken Egg Foo Yung as he said it was just like eating a chicken omelette. Anyway, as we were chatting and crossing the yard someone came past Dads place via the Back Lane wheeling a cooker on a wheelbarrow, we thought it was a strange time to be moving furniture around as it was about 11pm, anyway the next morning we found out that someone had broken into the house further down from Dads and had stolen the cooker and unbeknown to us we had witnessed more or less the whole incident!

Sometime afterwards, Dad managed to secure a tenancy with the Council and was allocated a one bedroomed Bungalow near to Auntie Marjorie and Uncle Timothy's, who as it happens, had also moved from their House into a Bungalow and not long afterwards my Auntie Beryl and Uncle Fletcher also moved house and had returned from Lancashire back to the village after buying a Bungalow which happened to be just along the road from both my Dad's place and my Auntie Marjorie's.

Dad's Bungalow was nice and had a garden where he used to grow vegetables. His next door neighbour was a pleasant little old lady who lived alone and Dad took it upon himself to always look out for her welfare which was nice as they were good neighbours to one another. Dads Sister's continued to keep an eye on him and he was doing really well emotionally even though Mam was still chipping away at him by sending letters or doing her secret telephone calls which disrupted his sleep pattern, he said that he thought that she was doing this so that it would upset him.

Now you know that I mentioned earlier that after Dad had moved back to the North-East and he used to shake, well although this had all but disappeared Dad still displayed a slight tremor in his hands and if his nerves got the better of him especially when we talked about Mam it made the tremor more pronounced. Had my Mam really made my Dad a nervous wreck? Hmm it's hard to forget the fact that these two people chose to be with one another and "Once Upon a Time" they gave each other the most precious of gifts ... Us! BUT isn't this the case in almost all divorces? I personally have never seen a supposed 'Amicable' break up yet!

Prior to this sometimes when Dad came to pick us up from either Warwickshire or Staffordshire we would travel to Lancashire for our holidays to his Sister Beryl's and Brother-in-Law Fletcher's house who I mentioned earlier. They had originally moved there with their two children Kenneth and Lynda and remained there until quite some considerable years later before returning to the North-East. We always loved going to their house and they used to make a real fuss of us plus we got on really well with our Cousins. Sometimes my best friend Polly would also be invited and we would spend the week taking really nice walks along the Canals and visiting Craft and Antiques Fairs which Dad absolutely loved. I loved my Auntie Beryl as she used to be so funny, infact I was saying to her recently that she just cracks me up with the things that she says, I loved spending time with my Uncle Fletcher too as he introduced me to the Singer Elkie Brooks and bought me her cassette tapes "Pearls and Pearls II" which were absolutely 'mint' Albums at the time, he was mad on her. During one of these holidays I can remember the Grown Ups going out for the night to see a Band called "The Dooley's" they were a Pop Group at the time that comprised of eight members, six of which were family members, they had several UK Chart Hits between 1977 and 1981 including several top ten hits including "Wanted", "Love of my Life" and "The Chosen Few". My Dad dressed for the night in a brand new bottle green velvet jacket that he looked a 'knockout' in; by heck he didn't half scrub up well and looked so handsome.

Other days out for us were to Dads younger Sister Kitty's and Brother-in-Law Ted's house. They had one child called Jessica who was younger than me and was really cute and nice, she loved my Dad too and we would always go for lovely walks in the countryside near to their house. I can always remember the stream that was to the back of their property which was amazing as it had open fields both to the front and rear of the house, really beautiful, it was just so lovely spending time with our family as they were lovely to be around; I have never doubted that they loved us. I have a photograph that I treasure of Jessica and me standing on either side of my Dad when we were on the beach in the North-East, he is in the middle of us holding each of our hands and you can see the wind whipping up my hair just as the photograph was taken, it takes pride of place on my Dresser and even now I find it hard to believe that this photograph was taken over thirty years ago. By now Kelvin and I were travelling to the North-East by National Express to see Dad and the journey was a very long one from Warwickshire, being 10 hours, this trip had the extra complication of us having to change buses in Oldham. I feel no shame in saying that I relied totally on my Brother to help me with this journey as I was terrified of missing the connection or getting lost, as you now know that was one of my biggest fears, thankfully even though we hated each other and fought all the time Kelvin used to look after me and the journey was a much better one for him being there. As we pulled into Durham Bus Station I would look out of the window and scan to see if Dad was there and I used to feel upset and anxious thinking that maybe he wouldn't be there but I needn't have worried and it was sheer joy to see him waiting for us, he never ever let us down, It's just a shame it wasn't like that on our return journey home as Mam couldn't be bothered to meet us at the Bus Station choosing instead to send Elliott. One time we waited for three hours in the freezing cold and we were starving hungry, in the end the Police took us home where we were faced with two drunken adults and I was well ticked off with them, I will probably tell you a little bit more about Elliott later on.

Another one of my homecomings I was shocked to see that Mam had been beaten black and blue and my entire bedroom door had been smashed in with a hammer. It was obvious that THEY had been fighting again and Mam had tried to lock herself in my bedroom and Elliott had supposedly gone crazy smashing a hammer repeatedly into my door, it looked a bloody mess I can tell you and really upset me as by now I started to worry about what would happen to Mam if I wasn't there, my heartstrings were well and truly being stretched to the limit especially when I was away visiting Dad.

It was about this time when my friend Wendy's Parents split up and her Dad had taken the split quite badly, after her Mum left Wendy remained with her Dad in the family home and her Dads reaction in order to cope with the breakdown of his marriage was to attempt to drink himself into an early grave. I suppose we formed a friendship because we were in similar circumstances and to try and take our minds off things we used to busy ourselves making mud pies and ashtrays in her greenhouse, we used to craft all sorts of things with the intention of letting the sun bake our creations. One night I attempted to open a red plastic bottle that was on one of the shelves inside the greenhouse when it suddenly exploded in my face leaving me covered in a dark substance which felt like it was burning my eyes and skin. It was some time later that it was identified as Tomato Plant Feeder which really stung; I had a really lucky escape and made a vow after that incident not to mess with stuff that didn't concern me. As it happens I chose Pottery as part of my Art course at High School and achieved a CSE1 which still brings a smile to my face, must have been all the practice I had had in Wendy's greenhouse.

Chapter 12

The Shame

Life became unsettled and very chaotic at times with Mam lying in bed all day while Kelvin and I got ourselves ready for school, the routine being that we took a breakfast tray up to her in bed, this being a pot of tea, two mugs which were each loaded with four and a half sugars and a drop of milk already in them and two slices of jam or lemon curd on bread. When we returned from school we never knew if we would be able to get into the house or not, if it was the latter we used to have to run around the village knocking on various houses to see if Mam was there, more often than not we used to locate her, well I say her but it was more like a set of keys at Elliott's Parent's house. His Mum by the way was lovely and we often had a chat with her while she was on her Postal Round, it's hard to believe that she gave birth to such a Monster. I shall tell you why I thought he was a Monster later on! On the 'locate the key' mission I would knock at the front door and after a while the upstairs bedroom window would be flung open and Elliott would lean out of the window and throw down our back door key. It is obvious to me now that Mam and Elliott were in bed and that he was actually naked as he wasn't wearing any clothes on the top half of his body when he appeared at the window. Once at home we would make a snack to eat, like Golden Syrup, Sugar, Jam or Lemon Curd on bread as we were now banned from touching the cooker as for reasons you well know. Afterwards we would go out to play, hours later just when it was turning dusk we would hear Mam shouting for us to come in and get ready for bed, "Kelvin ... Karina ..." we never had a problem hearing her voice, we could still hear her if we were playing three or four streets away! It was at about this time that Mam stopped shopping for groceries preferring instead to send one of us, I know this was the norm for a lot of kids, but our arms used to be dropping off with the weight of trying to carry 10lb of potatoes, a full vegetable order for the week plus all the other stuff, its sheer luck that Kelvin and I haven't got arms like an Orang-utan. Her cleaning routine was also beginning to slip, I don't mean that the standards of the house had gone down I just mean that by now Kelvin and I had to do chores before we left the house in a morning, one would wash, one would dry the dishes, one to polish the furniture and one to hoover the entire downstairs every day, this soon extended to cleaning our bedrooms and after a couple of years, went a stage further because every Tuesday night Kelvin had to empty the entire contents of the Pantry and scrub it out and I had to strip the Gas Cooker completely, scrub all the components and assemble it again. I know it sounds like I'm making a big deal of this but how many 15 year old boys would be doing that on a Tuesday night? Also the cleaning of the bedrooms was pretty intensive as every single week we used to have to pull all the furniture out, wipe the skirting boards with a soapy cloth, hoover behind and then wash the back of the each piece of furniture before putting them back. I did say she was obsessive to the point of us living in an almost sterile environment. As time moved on and the years passed, Kelvin and I became more and more fed up with the situation and we started to have really bad fights with one another about whose turn it was to do what and on one Saturday morning Kelvin decided to "wind me up" by saying that it was my turn to hoover when I knew it wasn't.

The argument went on and on until I completely lost my head and stamped my foot down onto the top of the hoover in sheer frustration, resulting in the hoover smashing "there, nobody's f****ing hoovering now"! I screamed. You know what Mam did? She broke down and cried over a bloody hoover for god sake, I was bloody fuming for a number of reasons as you can well imagine and well naffed off when I was given yet another chore to add to my 'to do' list ... the family ironing.

Now I have to take a deep breath so that I can tell you the rest of my story ... you see I was only 10 years old when my life changed forever and my childhood ended rather abruptly and the real world became a very ugly place.

One late night I heard loud music playing downstairs and I got up to go and tell Mam to turn it down but when I went into the living room there was only Elliott in there as Mam was apparently in bed and I had obviously made the mistake of assuming that it was her playing the music. Elliott told me that they had come back from a Fancy Dress Party and had argued resulting in Mam going to bed in the huff. He was dressed as a Russian Cossack and was very drunk and pleaded with me not to go, beckoning me over to the settee where he was lying down and indicated that I was to lie next to him, there was the strangest smell on his breath which I now know to be Pernod which to this day the sheer smell of this sickens me. He was telling me how much he loved being a part of our family and that he wouldn't hurt me and so on, apologies if this sounds so matter of fact but it is my way of coping with what happened next and to be quite honest this excuse of a man has taken enough of my life already and I will not allow him to take anymore. His time of being in control is no longer and if I could avoid this chapter of my life then I would but apart from this book helping me to face my Demons then I think it is only right to share the truth with you so here goes ... Elliott kissed me full on the lips ramming his tongue into my mouth, it was gross and he was scaring me, I struggled and was crying and he seemed to calm down for a few minutes until he guided my hand towards his penis which at the time I had no idea what it was, well apart from my Brother's pigeon but it was hardly in comparison to a fully erect penis. Time was moving at a slow snail's pace and my mind was racing, if only I had stayed in bed! I wanted my Mam to get this horrid excuse of a man away from me and I wanted my Dad to give him the biggest wallop of his life but in reality neither could help me ... He put his hand up my nightie and pulled my knickers down and proceeded to insert his finger inside me hurting my tiddly and making me sore on the inside in the process. I was horrified and hated him, this evil man was all over me, his horrid breath and hands touching me, his hands with fingernails that I can still visualise the shape of to this very day.

I didn't realise at the time but this was the first of many attacks to come, I just didn't know it yet, every opportunity that he had to abuse me he did and this seemed to go on for a very long time, probably most of the time that they were together. It didn't matter whether I was up or downstairs nothing deterred him. During his attacks I soon developed the art of letting my mind wander to the point where I must have looked vacant to an Outsider, this was after I discovered that I could not get away from him as he was just too strong so my thought was to just get it over with, how sad is that. It has taken me 37 years to say the following "I feel no shame in what happened to me, it wasn't MY fault" I know that now but I guess it has been easier for me over the years to just accept that this happened to me because I was a bad person and God was punishing me for something, a something that I couldn't work out the answer to. Anyway on the 9th August 2007 and I had reached the "Life begins at Forty" age I plucked up the courage to report Elliott to Social Services. This decision was hard as I had to summon all of my courage and strength to carry my decision through. After making the call my heart sank as I was informed that our Family Social Work files had apparently been destroyed the previous year and there was nothing more that I could do. I found it hard to accept that I had finally made it this far and all for nothing so I insisted on leaving my personal details with the Department with a view to coming forward if anyone else happened to report Elliott and that is how the situation stands to this day. I truly don't for one minute think that this is over as I have an overwhelming feeling that the day will come. I just have to hang on in there and remain strong, I am prepared to tell whoever wishes to listen what that Coward of a man did to me. He is a danger to any child as far as I am concerned and should be on the Sex Offenders Register. If you are reading this Elliott then you know who you are don't you, you know that YOU did these unforgiveable things to me don't you and I hope you will carry this guilt with you to your grave.

During this same time Social Services urged me to report Elliott to Warwickshire Police. They contacted Staffordshire Police and an appointment was made for me to meet with a Female Officer to discuss the abuse. When the Officer came to visit me I was told that the attacks had happened far too long ago and it would be hard for me to prove the allegations against him but I am a huge believer in that the truth will always win. I also find it hard to accept that Elliott for the moment is free but is this freedom a facade to the outside world? Surely with the things that he has done his mind cannot be free because it must eat at him to know that he has robbed someone else of any peace in their life? The Media today does nothing more than sensationalise the crimes of Jimmy Saville, Rolf Harris and Dave Lee Travis that is why I live in hope of someone else coming forward. I also know that this excuse of a man is now living in Shakespeare Avenue of all the places and sometimes I let my mind wander and dream of the day that I will go back and pass him in the street, it's not that I want to physically attack him, that would after all be too easy, I would just like to say the old cliché "Remember me"? Let me remind you of who I am and what you did to me when I was 10 years old you despicable excuse for a human being. I can't even justify calling him an animal, animals don't deserve this derogative comment, no it goes far deeper than that, to the point where there was never a limit to his unacceptable behaviour and I have since spent my life managing my heartache from the mental and physical abuse that he thrust upon me, you see I'm not even sure if I have dealt with this pain or if I have learned to live with it, either way it has reached the surface after being buried for most of my life. My pain takes me way back in my memory to the time when I went with Mia to Elliott's Parents house one afternoon to collect the key thinking that Mam was there but she wasn't, Elliott answered the door and beckoned us into the Living Room, a few minutes later I managed to establish that my Mam was not there and he didn't actually know where she was. He then asked me to go into the Hallway with him and for Mia to stay in the the other room as he was going to give each of us a surprise, I reluctantly followed him and soon discovered that this was just an excuse for him to abuse me much to my horror. After he had finished he told me to go back into the Living Room and to send Mia into him where I am pretty confident that much the same thing happened to her judging by the noises that I overheard but there was a huge difference, she didn't appear to object to what he was doing to her and because of this I soon left the house by the back door vowing never to return again, no matter what the circumstances were. Strange but Mia and I never discussed what had taken place that afternoon and she definitely sank further down in my estimations after all she was supposed to be my friend and I felt that she had betrayed me.

The abuse had a profound effect on me and I must have felt that I needed to prove to myself that I wasn't afraid of anything so for 'kicks' I took to sneaking around the Old Folks Home with my friend Debbie who lived just around the corner from my old Boyfriend Robin. The site consisted of a mixture of both Flats and Bungalows in a Retirement/Sheltered Housing complex and the gardens were lovely with wooden garden benches dotted all around which were smashing to hang around on. It was at this time that I thought I would give smoking a go, so Debbie and I used to rustle up the equivalent of 27.5 pence between us and off we would go to the VG shop to buy ten No.6 Tabs, back then, shops used to sell Tobacco and Alcohol to kids without question unlike today. We would return to the old folks place and sit on the benches and smoke these tabs like we were really cool and grown up. I wasn't even inhaling them as they tasted bloody awful but like I said I wanted to look cool. After a week of doing this I thought it would be great to smoke my five tabs one after the other, immediately afterwards I was violently sick and vowed to never touch a ciggie again. I think this rather immature adventure paid off in the long run though as I have never had the urge to smoke again.

One of the bad things that I also did during this particular summer was to go sniping (obviously been watching too many of my Dads war films). I would crawl over the grassed areas beneath the windows of the elderly residents doing a full circuit of the place and finally finishing in the washing line compound where I would have to scale a six foot white slatted fence to escape, my bravery went one stage further when I used to go into the stairwells of the flats and pretend that I was visiting my Grandma. God I must have been really bored and today I thank my lucky stars that I never frightened any of the Elderly Residents, to be honest if this had been the case I would have been mortified.

Chapter 13

Up on the Roof – (The Drifters)

The second Fire Brigade incident that I promised to tell you about earlier was when Mam and Elliott's relationship was nearing the end and they had returned home rather the worse for wear from a daytime drinking session at The Raven. The timing of this incident must have coincided with Mams decision to move us across the City to a God awful place. She had agreed that we would move in with a bloke called Ray who was the Chap I was telling you about that used to masquerade as a Policeman.

Apparently a violent row between Mam and Elliott had erupted which resulted in him chasing her upstairs where she managed to lock herself away in Kelvin's bedroom which as it happened at the time was stripped bare of all furniture leaving just a pile of tea chests ready for the pending move. I was on my way home with Mia and as we were chatting until I became slightly distracted by a commotion of some sort that was going on in our cul-de-sac, I soon came to a grinding halt just in time to witness the 'rescue' via a Fire Engine ladder which was in the process of extending out towards the roof of our house and towards ... my Mam. If you think that this was bad enough wait until I tell you what she was wearing ... yes my Mam was on the roof of our house wearing just a pair of Knickers and a Bra. By the time I managed to push through the rather large crowd that had gathered outside the house my Mam had been 'rescued' and I went inside to find her but I couldn't see her anywhere. The house was by now full of Emergency Service Personnel, I still could not find her until a Policeman kindly guided me towards my Mam who was sitting in the armchair to the left of the living room door. I still could not see her immediately as her face was totally covered in dried blood and was providing the effect of camouflage. Afterwards I looked around the house trying to determine what was salvageable and was pleasantly surprised as our belongings looked to be still in good shape, that is, until I got to Kelvin's room. It was a horrid sight and made me feel very frightened as there was blood splattered all over the white wallpaper and floorboards, infact it looked more like a scene from the film Psycho and if things couldn't get any worse some of the blood was still wet. I went back downstairs to Mam who was in the process of being stretchered out towards the Ambulance and asked her what had happened, she said that when Elliott had tried to leave the house she had opened Kelvin's bedroom window which was directly above the front door and had dropped a bottle of QC Sherry straight onto his head. With a direct hit achieved Elliott raced up the stairs to try and get to Mam, he ended up kicking the bedroom door in and gave her a severe beating, her only choice of escape was through the window and up onto the roof. Now this is where I can tell you about my link with Leicester.

By now life meant that our usual bedtime routine was followed by Kelvin and I being woken from our sleep by the sound of loud music and raised voices coming from downstairs and more often than not I would get up and wander downstairs into the living room where the radiogram would be blaring and there would be a room full of people. The room would be filled with cigarette smoke and the smell of booze, our Mam was having a great time with all of her newly acquired friends partying to Queen and 'Bohemian Rhapsody', Simon & Garfunkel's 'The Boxer', Cilla Black's 'Step inside Love', Kate Bush's 'Wuthering Heights', Donna Summers 'I feel love' and T Rex 'I Love to Boogie' and various Bee Gees and Barry White numbers which were frequently being belted out to name but a few. You see it wasn't just the parties that bothered me, it was Mam's dancing too, in my opinion she was outrageous on the dance floor particularly when Donna Summer's "I feel love" came on. I think that she used to go way too far and somehow used to give out the wrong signals to the fella's to the point of her being totally embarrassing, I wonder now if she was ever challenged by anyone's Wife or Girlfriend for 'coming onto' their other half either way she used to make me feel uncomfortable.

Sometimes during Mam's parties there would be the sound of things being smashed, followed by screaming and shouting and it wasn't long before I was able to identify the noise of my Mam when she was being physically attacked. By this time her so called Guests would hurriedly leave and Mam would shout and cry out for Kelvin to go to her in-between each 'thud' or 'slap' and after months and months of this happening Kelvin just stopped responding to her calls choosing to stay in bed instead. You know writing this down it doesn't sound too bad but you had to be a part of it to understand the trauma that we felt, hearing your Mam being physically attacked and verbally abused was horrific and I know it used to leave me physically shaking in my bed to the point where I would either cry myself to sleep or I would go down to her. It was on one of these occasions that I thought I would be brave and try to sneak down and escape from the house so that I could call the Police. Unfortunately, I was cornered in the Hallway by Elliott, he was really angry and was swearing at me, he then lifted me up with one hand by clasping me around my throat so that my feet were dangling about a foot from the floor, the other hand he screwed up into a fist and threatened to slam it into my face and break my nose. Mam begged him to put me down but he kept me dangling there for a few minutes while she tried to negotiate with him. I cannot find the words to describe how I felt at that moment as I think I just felt numb and after what seemed an absolute age he snarled at me to "get back to bed" and I ran as fast as I could up to my bedroom where I lay quivering in my bed while he continued to beat my Mam. The fight continued for at least a further two hours and the intensity of the noise coming from downstairs is one that I cannot describe, by now I was asking God what I had done that was so bad that he had to punish me? I just couldn't find the answer to my question and felt totally let down by God and his Heaven after all if he loved me like I loved him he wouldn't have wanted me to feel all the pain surely? As a consequence I never bothered going to Sunday School after that as it was just a stupid waste of time, anyway I was only going for the free beaker of orange squash and the free biscuit so it didn't really matter to me as it wasn't like I was missing out on anything as surely nothing else bad could happen to me?

Things did not change or improve and it was particularly bad one summer holidays to the point where I no longer slept in bedclothes but chose instead to stay dressed in a pair of shorts and vest so that I could make a quick exit if I needed to. I used to put my flip flops at the side of the bed in case I needed to make a quick getaway and summon help from the police. One morning Mia's Mum said "I heard your little feet last night running past our house at about 2am". Well, woman why didn't you bloody report my Mam and bring this nightmare to a bloody end, or had she already reported what was going on but had got nowhere? Night after night the same situation with me running around to the Shopping Precinct and calling the Police from the Telephone Box and being told by them to wait for a Panda Car to pick me up. Gladly I only had to wait a few minutes for their arrival. During these times I used to stand and worry myself almost to the point of vomiting as I was fretting so much about what would be waiting for me when I got home. I felt so bloody hopeless when I got there as Mam would say to the Police that everything was fine, no problem or Elliott had already left the property even though she would be sporting a split lip, broken nose or black eye that had already started to close up and impair her vision. This life was stressing me out and I felt really nervous all the time to the point that I did something that I had never done before and that was that I wet the bed, just the once, but it had such a massive impact on me and as a result my self-esteem hit an all-time low to the point that I felt like I was becoming a nervous wreck. It reached the stage where I couldn't stand the television or radio being played loudly and couldn't stay in the house unless all the interior doors were closed throughout the house, even to the point where still to this day I will not sleep close to the bedroom door. I always have to be facing the door just in case someone tries to attack me, surely this isn't right.

I would like say that to the outside world it was quite obvious by now that something was going on with us as a family, for example, you only had to watch us play, I can remember the time when Mam bought me a Tiny Tears Doll and cot which were all the rage at the time and I was really cross with her choice as it wasn't my thing to play with Dolls anymore, what was the point. When my cousin Dionne came to visit, she also had an identical Doll which she played the 'Mummy' to carrying her Doll everywhere and wrapping it up cradling it gently to her. What about me, what was I doing with my 'baby'? Firstly I stood inside the cot and put my foot through the floor of it in sheer frustration and then I pulled the arms and legs off the Doll in utter disgust. Not long after this incident I received a parcel through the post for my Birthday. Dad had sent me a Sindy Doll which came with its very own bed, which I think my Auntie Marjorie had helped Dad to choose. It had all the bed clothes, pillow and sheets and Sindy had some clothes to change into and the whole gift would have been wonderful for any other 'normal' little girl but sadly I was no longer 'normal' I was damaged but damaged in a way that I couldn't understand

and this confusion made me feel like the sunshine had gone out of my little world. By now we were no longer receiving the gifts of money from our family in the North-East due to Mam using it to fund her partying! Anyway back to the story of Sindy ... I swiftly put a noose around the neck of Sindy and suspended her from underneath the seat of the dining chair where she hung for days following her execution, from then on I played with my Brother's Action Man preferring the thought that at least that had all manner of weapons and accessories to help it out of whatever situation presented itself. Was this the start of me fearing the worst to come and was this my way of acting out my preparations for the worst dilemma through the Action Man? It wasn't long after this that Kelvin and I received two silver St. Christopher Pendants through the post from our Auntie Marjorie and Uncle Timothy. Maybe it was their way of reaching out to us in the hope of keeping us safe either way we treasured them.

At regular times I caught Mam having sex with Elliott in the Living Room of our house, it was not a nice thing to see and hear and I struggled emotionally to understand this intimate act particularly following the violence that Elliott constantly dished out. Sometimes I was spared walking in on them as the armchair would be pushed up against the Living Room door, this left me feeling isolated and very confused as I wrestled with the fact of whether this was an acceptable thing to be doing or not?

Let me share with you another Brother story ... Kelvin came rushing into the house excited that he had found a secret under the hedge in the playing fields. Apparently he and his friend Taffy had been playing over the field when they spotted two black bin liners which appeared to have been shoved under the hedge. When they peeked inside they found that they were full of cigarettes and when they came back to tell Mam what they had found she insisted that the Boys showed her where the bags were. So under Mam's instruction they promptly brought the bags back to the house where Mam proceeded to bribe my Brother and Taffy with a cash reward telling them that they had only found the "dummy" cigarette boxes that they used for display purposes in shop windows. She must have thought that we were really stupid as why would she bribe them if they were worthless. Following this she soon let the 'cat out of the bag' because every Visitor to our house was offered a Cigarette or Cigar from a wooden ornamental box which seemed to have every brand known to man in it. This was a particularly foolish thing to do as Mam was now claiming the *Nash and clearly could not afford this luxury and not long afterwards we heard that someone had robbed the local VG shop and had got away with a substantial quantity of cigarettes, Mam being Mam still could not keep this low key and when we were invited to our Cousin's Wedding the first thing she did when she went into the Reception Hall was to put a handful of cigarettes on each table for the guests to help themselves, talk about drawing attention to yourself, this is how blatant she was though and do you know what?

She still got away with it!

Things went from bad to worse and desperate times presented as by now the Coal Board had stopped delivering Dad's Coal Allowance to our house and we were freezing. We could not light the fire in the Breakfast Room which would have enabled us to have had not only a source of heating but also hot water as the fire also heated the back boiler. I decided to take it upon myself to scour the local fields and woodlands on a daily basis for dead wood to burn and it was at this time that I also learnt the skill of identifying Wild Fungi enabling me to pick field Mushrooms which I took home and Mam cooked. Wild mushrooms grew abundantly all over the fields close to our house and they were especially plentiful growing in the middle of cow pats, it was an art in itself trying to extract them from the pat without getting cow muck on your hands even more so as I did not have any tools to assist me. The only other

* Nash – Geordie word for Social Security.

source of heating in our house was the gas fire which was in the living room but Mam only put this on for short periods of time because of the cost of the gas bill. One time being Sunday night which was traditionally bath night and where Mam used to lather me and Kelvin with a foul smelling, highly flammable head lice treatment which was turquoise coloured, we wouldn't have minded if we had actually got head lice but we hadn't and to add insult to injury she then used to make us sit in front of the gas fire of all places to supposedly dry off, how we didn't go up in flames I'll never know.

Bath night brings so many memory's back to me especially as there was an art to getting in and out of our bath unscathed as Mam used to scrub it clean with Vim and the rinsing off process was never ending, needless to say that once you slid into the bath it felt like your buttocks were sliding against sandpaper such was the feeling of putting naked skin against the grit residue left behind from the Vim. The other annoying thing that she did was that every time I went in the bath she used to scrub my knees, elbows and knuckles with a hard nail brush, the reason for this ... Because I have olive coloured skin and she said that I looked filthy! Oh and more pain to come when she used to stick her very long little finger nail in my *lugs to get the *taties out and clean them. When Kelvin and I were much younger we used to go into the bath together (funny how I always ended up at the tap end and if I protested he used to hit me). Mam never failed to ask us if I had washed my tiddly and if Kelvin had washed his pigeon? To this day I have never had the courage to try pigeon pie, can you blame me. Sometimes it was not possible to have a bath at home and we would have to go over to Shaky Jed's to use his bath, he lived across the road and was a really nice Chap. Sometimes I would go and collect a bucket of coal from his bunker and take it home, his wife Carol had run off with another bloke and had taken their two kids with her which had left him feeling

---

* Lugs – Geordie word for ears.

* Taties – Geordie word also meaning ear wax.

devastated. I'm not sure what the arrangement was with Mam and Jed for the use of the bath or the coal and I kind of never wanted to ask as it may have just been kindness on his part. It got so bad over the bath situation that Mam got our old baby bath out of the Loft and we went back to the days of having a bath in front of the gas fire a bit like the old Miner's would have done, how embarrassing trying to maintain your privacy with not only my Mam but also my Brother who kept bursting into the living room, this annoying thing that he persisted on doing left me quivering in the bath. It was bad enough trying to fit in to the bloody thing without everything else going on ... Kelvin!

During this time one of the things that Mam tried to get us to eat was something she called Boiley, which I have to say, is totally gross but at the time she made it sound like we were about to eat Caviar. We must have been really struggling with money for her to resort to this but all the same we tried Mam's version of this dish which was a combination of white bread which she had broken into small pieces and placed in a bowl, boiling milk was poured over the top and finally sugar sprinkled on the top which resulted in the most awful concoction of sloppy bread. To this day I cannot stomach the thought of eating Bread and Butter pudding due to the consistency.

Now before you go jumping to any conclusions and thinking that Dad just left us to fend for ourselves you will sadly be mistaken, he was so proud of the fact that from the day he returned to the rest of our family in the North-East he paid £16 per week (£8 per child) Maintenance and the only time he failed briefly to do this was in 1984 during the Miner's Strike and even then he tried to pay for as long as he could using his Savings in the hope that it would tide him over. Hmm now to put this into some kind of perspective ... during this time in the 1970's an average weekly wage was around £32, you could buy a house for around £5000, a brand new Mini £600, loaf of bread cost nine pence, trip to the Cinema for two less than ninety pence, 20 tabs were twenty pence and a pint of beer just twenty pence so £16 was a lot of money. Dad was proud that he was our Father and he never ever shirked any of his responsibilities to us, he didn't want us to ever go without. The UK's Miner Strike by the way lasted until 1985 and brought about hardship for many of the workers so much so that two local unsigned bands called The Pigeon Fanciers and Haswell Crisis recorded and released a Single to both raise money for the families and to recognise the contribution made by the Miner's over the years in their locality. Their adapted version of a Bob Dylan classic failed to Chart but the project made a slight profit as local support from other mining communities ensured that 'Knocking on ******'s Floor' sold in excess of 1000 copies.

Chapter 14

The Dying Fly – (Tiswas)

My Auntie Margaret, Uncle Derek and four Cousins, Lyndsay, Clare, Donya and Dionne moved from our village to a town in Leicester. They managed to buy their very own four bedroomed semi-detached house which had a garage, driveway and front and back gardens which at the time was quite an achievement for an ex-Miner to do. My Uncle Derek had left the Pit by now and had secured a job with Rolls Royce Aerospace and my Auntie Margaret got a job in the Catering Department at the local Hospital. They both worked hard to save and make the best of their home which was their pride and joy, Lyndsay and Clare helped out a lot by looking after their two younger Sisters so that their Parents could work extra hours.

The house always looked lovely and must have at some point in its life had Servants because there were Service Bells in each room with the main Control Box being located in the large room off the Scullery, also in this room lived Sparky, he was the family Budgie and used to scare the pants off me especially when my Cousin Dionne let him out of his cage into the room where he liked nothing better than to stretch his wings, he used to say his name which sounded so strange.

Auntie Margaret was very house proud and as such everything gleamed from her constant cleaning routine, I think she had the biggest collection of brass ornaments that I have ever seen which she proudly displayed in the huge display cabinets which were in both Reception rooms of the house. Uncle Derek was always lovely to us even though he was quite strict with his girls, I wonder if this was because he became "the man of the house" at a very early age after his Father had passed away, I believe he was a Teenager when this happened and left him with the huge responsibility of looking out for his Mother and Sister Janet? We would often travel the fifteen miles over to their house so that Mam and Dad could socialise with my Auntie and Uncle, Dad liked nothing more than to go for a game of Snooker with Uncle Derek. While the Grown Ups were out we used to sit in the living room at the front of the house watching the television with our cousins, Donya used to make us run a comb up and down her arm tickling her, we had to count to one hundred before it was her turn to do it to us and you could often hear protests from one of us "You're counting too quick or that's not fair"!. That apart we all got on really well together and I think that Kelvin was very brave spending all evening with us five girls; the highlight of the evening was when our Parents returned from their night out with a treat for all of us ... Bags of KP salted peanuts!

Dionne used to like to play the game Mousetrap with me and I was fascinated with the set-up of this particularly when the Trap was triggered and the Mouse finally caught. We always used to be playing a Board Game or Hide and Seek or something like that and if I was to be honest there was never enough hours in the day for us to spend with our Cousins as the time just flew by.

Now the strange thing was that even though I always had a lovely time at our Cousins house I was scared of going anywhere in their house on my own as it was enormous having two large Reception rooms, one at the front which I have already mentioned and one at the back that had a beautiful, claret red carpet and Georgian style French Doors leading out into the private back garden which had a mixture of tall fencing and hedges. My Auntie Margaret used to love to sunbathe in the garden and we would often find her stretched out on one of her sun loungers just lapping up the sun.

The house also had an enormous Hallway which connected the rooms from the front of the house to the back and the Scullery which was painted blue and had a twin sink and large preparation area where the Dining Room led off, from here a deep step leading down into a narrow walk in Pantry that had all manner of foodstuffs stored in there. Back into the Hall and underneath the staircase was an alcove where all the coats and shoes were stored, this area became a favourite place for my Cousin Dionne to hide and just as I would be walking past she would leap out from behind the coats and scare the life out of me. At the bottom of the staircase they had a black Candlestick telephone which stood proudly upon a telephone shelf; this must have been really old as I had never seen one like it before. Up the stairs was Donya and Dionne's bedroom to the right which they shared, opposite this the large family bathroom, Auntie Margaret and Uncle Derek's bedroom was on the front of the property, their room seemed enormous to the point where their double bed looked lost in there. In the opposite direction along a narrow corridor and through an archway towards the rear of the property were Clare's and then Lyndsay's bedrooms which were always neat and tidy, nothing dared to be out of place, mind you now I think of it this was the case throughout the entire house.

My Uncle Derek always used to prefer to drive an Automatic Transmission car and I can remember a white car that he had which I thought was either a Humber or Ford Zephyr, I'm not sure which. One of the cars had seating for six people and the three older girls would sit in the back of the car leaving Dionne who would sit in-between her Parents on a seat which was identical to the rear one. I can distinctly remember that the seats were covered in a red vinyl type material which gave the impression of them looking very similar to leather. By the way travelling with any of my Cousins was not advisable as all four of them were terribly car sick, to the point where they each used to have to carry a plastic bucket on journeys and I can remember feeling rather smug as this was not something that either Kelvin or I suffered with.

Can you remember the incident with Mam being rescued from the roof top? Well it was situations like that that resulted in Kelvin and me going to stay with Auntie Margaret and Uncle Derek as Mam would have either been beaten so badly that she was admitted to Hospital or she had taken yet another overdose, plus on the odd occasion Mam would pretend to be having a Tachycardia episode, which for those of you not familiar with this is also called Supraventricular Tachycardia (SVT) and is the name given to an abnormality of heart rhythm, characterised by a fast heartbeat and this would also always end in Mam being admitted to Hospital. Anyway, for whatever reason, we were always driven in a Police car over to our family in Leicester where they took us in and looked after us for usually a week or so at a time, something that I will always be grateful to them for, and I know that Kelvin feels the same gratitude towards our Auntie and Uncle as this can't have been easy for any of them as we must have disrupted the routine of the household greatly. I really admire them though as they never had a bad word to say about us and they always made us feel that they wanted us there even though there would be six kids to feed at mealtimes, six for the bath and a hell of a lot of washing, so yes they certainly did their best for us and I will always be grateful to them. Not sure if I mentioned earlier that Brother and Sister from my family married Brother and Sister from another local family, so in plain terms my Auntie

Margaret married Derek and my Uncle Edgar married Derek's Sister Janet.

My Uncle Edgar and Auntie Janet lived in North Yorkshire with my Cousins Jackie, Pauline and Greg and we all used to get on really well together, infact I can't remember any Cousins that we didn't get along with. I'm not sure if this is a common occurrence you know Brother and Sister marrying Brother and Sister but I personally have never come across this before or since.

This leads me nicely into Family Celebrations and Mam's atrocious behaviour to the point where both Kelvin and I used to dread attending, either way we were a large family with lots of occasions to celebrate much to our horror. Now let me think … it was either my Cousin Edwin's or Jeffrey's wedding and the Reception was held in a Hall which was close to our village. Mam did her usual and got so drunk at the Reception afterwards, it all got really embarrassing and I could see my Grandma Greta getting anxious while looking on and after scanning the room I was relieved to see some of my family debating in hushed tones on how best to handle the situation, curb her behaviour and rescue the celebration, but this in itself was difficult as nobody wanted to cause a scene. A short while later after drinking more booze Mam did the "Piece de Resistance" and took to the dance floor after requesting the DJ to play the "Dying Fly Dance"! This crazy dance was shown on Tiswas "Today is Saturday Watch and Smile" which was broadcasted on a Saturday morning from 1974 to 1982 for Kids and hosted by Chris Tarrant, Sally James and Lenny Henry. The dance involved people lying on their backs on the floor and waving their arms and kicking their legs in the air, needless to say that my Mam was the only person on the dance floor and I tried my hardest to make myself invisible.

Kelvin on the other hand had other ideas for entertainment, a family member caught him carrying a tray of champagne outside and when they questioned him as to where he was going he told them he was taking them out to the Band who were having a short break on the car park. A little while later my Granda asked why Kelvin was outside and the response was "Oh he's just talking to the Band on the Car Park", my Granda said there is no Band, it's a Disco! By the time they caught up with Kelvin he was merrily enjoying himself with the tray of drinks, his first experience of drinking ... Bless!

As the years passed my relationship with my Brother had changed slightly for the better and I can only liken our relationship to the Brother and Sister that starred in the 1991 film "The Prince of Tides" as it reminds me so much of us. The film is a romantic drama film starring Barbara Streisand as a Psychiatrist called Susan Lowenstein and Nick Nolte as a Teacher and Football Coach called Tom Wingo and is about the struggle to overcome psychological damage inflicted on him and his Sister during their childhood in South Carolina. In the film Tom's Mother Lila asks him to go to New York to help his twin Sister's Psychiatrist Lowenstein after his Sister Savannah's latest suicide attempt. After Tom meets with Lowenstein he is reluctant to disclose many details about their childhood but tells her that their Father who was a successful Shrimp Boat Operator was also a brute of a man who spent all the family money on hair brained business ventures leaving the family in poverty. Tom reveals that when they were 13 years old, three escaped Convicts sought refuge in the family home and raped him, Savannah and his Mother. His older Brother Luke shoots two of the Convict's dead with a shotgun and the third is stabbed to death by Lila with a kitchen knife, they bury the bodies underneath the house and never spoke about it again. It is an amazing film and if you have never seen it then make sure you do. It was nominated for seven Academy Awards including Best Picture but lost the award to The Silence of the Lambs.

My Brother and I were present when we had two break-ins in our house; this is why the memory reminds me so much of the film. Is this because maybe we held so much of our abuse inside ourselves not knowing how to deal with it or more to the point make any sense of it, maybe not, but I've spent years trying to find the answers to the one BIG question, WHY US??? Why did our lives have to be so painful? I know my Brother has asked this question too but neither of us can find the answer no matter how hard or deep we look back, and that is the one major thing we have in common, it's our invisible bond you see.

During one of Mam's nights out she left Kelvin and I watching the television in the Living Room (in those days you didn't have televisions in bedrooms), sometime later we heard a strange noise coming from the back of the property towards the Scullery. We quickly and rather reluctantly mustered up the courage to sneak towards the Breakfast Room to take a peek, it sounded like someone was trying to break in through the back door. Kelvin and I were terrified and made our way upstairs as fast as we could, once upstairs Kelvin beckoned me to him and whispered for me to hide in the little cupboard that was in my room, he then crossed back across the Landing and hid himself behind the toilet door. I sat patiently on the laundry boiler which was in the cupboard and looked down at how pathetic I must have looked sitting there in just my nightie. I felt so utterly vulnerable, I managed to peek through the tiny gap in the door and frame so I could see if anyone came into my room, I could hear someone searching downstairs and then focusing their attention on the upstairs. In the meantime I was trying not to cry and also trying not to breathe noisily but this was proving to be really difficult as I was scared. Luckily for us whoever was in our house only went into Mam's bedroom where we later discovered that they had emptied the contents of her black lacquered, oriental style musical jewellery box and took what they could. I would like to say "Thank you Kelvin" for taking care of me that night and putting me first to the point of compromising your own safety. When we next saw our Dad we told him about the incident and also disclosed that Mam's engagement ring which he had bought for her had been stolen, he was convinced that our Mam had set the whole thing up? I honestly don't know whether this was the case or not, if it was it was a really stupid thing to do considering her two Bairns were at home and anything could have gone wrong with the so called plan!

Not long afterwards Kelvin and I had to deal with another break in as Mam and Boyfriend Elliott had fallen out and as such she had decided to lock him out of the house which he was none too pleased about, he decided to smash one of the panes of glass through on the front door and let himself in, once inside he beat the crap out of Mam. The next morning we waited for Elliott to leave before Kelvin and I went to the Hardware shop where we bought some laths of wood similar to roofing laths and took them home. Kelvin got Dads hammer and nails and nailed each strip of wood around the edge of the door so that it was nailed shut, he then fixed a piece of hardboard over the broken pane of glass and finally used a carving knife to cut a rectangular shape out to accommodate the letter box, even if Elliott smashed the hardboard through, there was no way he was getting in the house through the door and he couldn't gain entrance through the back door as it had a big bolt at the bottom of it which was completely out of his reach even if he smashed a pane of glass through. Mam then urged us to hide all the sharp knives and tools including the hammer and screwdrivers in the garden so that Elliott could not use them to hurt us with so we dug a hole and buried everything inside it. There was a real sense of urgency as we were worried we would not get everything done in time before Elliott returned and like I said I think Mam just wanted to get anything that could be used as a weapon out of the way. The really strange thing about this particular day was that we were now working together as a team and it felt odd as it was just like Mam had always been that way with us, it was a shock to me when I realised this as we had never done anything like this with our Mam before. That night all three of us sat tight in the Living Room with the lights out and the television off and all was well so we decided to go to bed sometime near to midnight. I must have quickly fallen asleep but something suddenly roused me, I tried to listen and could hear Mam talking downstairs to someone so I went downstairs to investigate. I went into the Living Room to find Mam standing at the open window talking to Elliott who was in our front garden. She was wearing just a cream nylon petticoat and from what I could gather the jist of the conversation was that she was refusing to let him into the house, well done Mam, stay strong for all of us!! The relief I felt when Mam refused to give in to Elliott's sweet talking was overwhelming and I felt a huge weight lift from my shoulders, yes, all three of us had won this battle and my Brother's first attempt at DIY was a complete success! Unfortunately, my elation was short-lived as sometime after we had all returned to bed we were woken again by some sort of commotion coming from our Mam's bedroom. I sprang out of bed half asleep only to meet my Brother on the Landing as we both made our way into Mam's room to see what all the drama was about and were horrified to see Elliott forcing his way in through the bedroom window with the aid of a set of aluminium ladders which he had obviously borrowed from one of our neighbouring properties. Kelvin and I immediately backed out of the room and went back to our beds where we listened to him beat Mam really badly. We were both helpless to stop this after all we were no match against this man and as a result of this we both admitted defeat. It seemed that we would just have to accept that Elliott was invincible and our situation was totally hopeless.

Chapter 15

Another One Bites the Dust – (Queen)

Somewhere along the line Mam met another chap called Dom who was a Widower. He lived in a really nice swanky house (not a Pit house) on a posh estate somewhere in Warwickshire and drove a lovely navy blue Triumph Dolomite. It was obvious to us that this guy had money and as such it was clearly one of the attributes that Mam had been drawn to. We started staying over at his place at the weekends where we were quickly introduced to his Mother, Daughter and his dog which was a white Poodle. Dom's Mother was really nice and obviously had a lot of input in the home as it was always kept lovely, she used to do his shopping and also spend a huge amount of time with her Granddaughter particularly as she only lived up the street. Her Granddaughter by the way had long strawberry blonde hair and lots of freckles and was a real pig to me when we were in the privacy of her bedroom she laughed at my clothes particularly my white socks as they had taties in, she was a snooty little Madam in my eyes and had no business being mean to me, after all I hadn't been mean to her. Thankfully Dom and his Mother were always nice to us and I never felt uncomfortable around them, I'm not sure why but Mam's relationship ended quite quickly with Dom and afterwards she met a bloke called Ray.

We didn't really know much about Ray or how Mam and him came to meet one another, all we knew was that his ex-Wife had left him and taken their two boys to live with her and they apparently lived somewhere nearby but Ray didn't seem to have any contact with his Son's and apart from that I can't tell you anymore about them other than they had blonde hair and lots of freckles and I only knew this because I saw a school photograph of them. One day after school, I was told we were moving to Ray's house which was the other side of the City. I had no idea where this idea had come from but Mam said that we were going and there would be no negotiation no matter how much both Kelvin and I protested, neither of us wanted to move to a strange place or new school particularly without any friends and to a place completely alien to us, could life get any worse? Besides which I had no idea where exactly she was taking us especially as I had never heard of the place before, she just might as well have said we were moving to the Moon!

Ray lived in a three bedroomed house in a cul-de-sac in an area that didn't seem to be too nice particularly as it was built up, no nice fields or woods to play in, more like a really unpleasant area to be in so much so that it felt to me like I couldn't breathe in the place. The thing that stood out to me when I first moved there was the amount of Black and Indian people that lived there as I had only seen one Black person before and that was Dancing Davy who I mentioned earlier.

There wasn't time to say goodbye to our friends and I got the impression that we were doing a moonlight flit to avoid Elliott and whether that was the case or not we were getting out of the village and we were getting out quick!

Ray's house had a downstairs bathroom, living room and kitchen and three bedrooms which were upstairs, there was nothing in the house in the way of carpets or furniture as apparently Ray's ex Wife had taken most of the carpets and furniture with her and the boys when she had walked out on him, that is apart from a rather naff looking sideboard that was covered in a type of fablon which was in the style of a mock wood grain and also some ornamental wall weaponry. Ray's ex Wife did however leave the cat behind but even that turned out to be a dirty little thing as every time I got up in a morning to go and have a wash and a cup of tea it had either shit in the kitchen sink or in the bath, why would a cat do that? To add insult to injury we had been made to leave our cat Kitty behind so I was not impressed at all.

Soon after we moved, Mam took us to the local schools where I was devastated to be told that I would infact be missing my final year in Junior School and instead enrolling straight into the local High School. I was devastated with this latest decision and very frightened as I didn't feel in any way, shape or form that I was ready for this move and I was worried to the point of fretting and I don't think that my Brother was very happy either. Kelvin and I had to wear bottle green V neck jumpers, Kelvin grey trousers and me a grey skirt which I totally hated as I never wore skirts or dresses anymore, choosing rather to wear things that I felt more secure in as anything else just left me feeling very vulnerable as far as I was concerned, I had the same feeling or insecurities with nighties too, pyjamas being the much better option.

My first day at the new school I met a very quiet girl called Colette who was extremely thin (even thinner than me) almost anorexic looking and we became friends but still I never really settled, hating every moment I was there and feeling more and more unhappy and withdrawn, none of our family visited us while we lived there and I guess that by now I was feeling more and more lost and alone. I no longer went out to play and can't recall having anyone call around to ask me to play, instead, I would spend some of my free time sitting in the MG Spitfire that was parked up in the Ray's garage which I think was possibly an unfinished project of his. My world had well and truly turned upside down and I was extremely unhappy even though Mam went about putting her personal mark on the house with all of our belongings from the old place and even though the downstairs was made to feel homely I cannot remember her putting any effort into my bedroom as it only had foam underlay on the floor and my chest of drawers and double bed only went a small way into trying to furnish the room and guess what? My purple curtains were far too small for the window and were more of a decoration rather than actually functioning properly, no wonder I had no interest in anything and it was soon obvious that Mam had made yet another bad decision and although it may have been to get away from Elliott she went about things in the wrong way having no regard for either Kelvin's or my feelings.

Ray's Parents lived close by and they tried to make us feel welcome, the only trouble being that I didn't trust Ray's Dad as he was always dropping around to the house in his electric blue coloured Mini Car when Mam wasn't in and he made me feel totally uncomfortable. He had a walking stick to help him with his balance which was a bit 'iffy' due to the fact that he had a built up shoe and something called a 'club foot'. On one occasion he picked me up and drove me over to his bungalow but on the way he made an attempt to feel my right leg as he supposedly struggled to change gear, he wasn't very subtle and once we arrived at his bungalow I was relieved to see his Wife was waiting for me with tea and cake. He rather bizarrely tried to get me to sit on his lap which was so not happening and I can remember thinking oh no not another dirty old man. I couldn't understand how he could be like that especially in front of his lovely Wife. After six months we were on the move again with Ray now in tow. I don't know how she did it but she had him moving with us back to Staffordshire where his stay happened to be very short-lived.

Dad had been picking us up and dropping us back off when we were going away with him for the week and it was during this time that Mam started to play up to Dad by making us all feel really uncomfortable when she was around him. It got to the stage where Dad didn't dare get out of the car and see us to the door with our suitcase as Mam would try and engage him into making another go of things, you see, I was upset enough when Dad brought me back and would cry for a week afterwards wanting to be with him to the point where it must have done her head in and she used to say things like "your Dad's a Bastard" and so on.

Our move to Staffordshire was not to be our last move as we had only been offered a two bedroomed ground floor flat to rent in Westminster Avenue which also just so happened to back onto a local beauty spot. I'm not sure how or why we were allocated this property as Kelvin and I would have been 12 and 14, therefore I don't think that we should have been sharing a bedroom together at that age, either way we were and guess what? I was back on that bloody bottom bunk again in the tiniest of bedrooms with my trusty old purple curtains hanging at the window! Can you imagine me and Kelvin sharing airspace in such a confined area, it did little to help our relationship I can tell you! Apart from the issue with the bedroom the flat was nice and Mam made a good job of making it a home, we couldn't afford a carpet in the Hall or Living room and 'made do' with carpet runners which in turn presented my Brother and I with yet another chore ... We had to take it in turns polishing the floor tiles that surrounded our carpet offcuts with a liquid polish that came in a bottle similar to washing up liquid, this job was tedious I can tell you and if my Grandma Greta could have seen me on my hands and knees she would have thought that I had travelled back in time and was working 'in service'.

One night Mam went out for a night with the local Girls, the Girls being our neighbours Isla and Cathy and she left Ray at home, on their return it was clear to see that they had all had a really good night and everything appeared to have gone well, that is until we discovered that Mam had also brought a little something extra home from the pub ... A Bloke that we had never seen before, infact he was the 'Rag and Bone' man! See I told you there was no shame in her and the aftermath for us was obvious ... we had the mickey taken out of us from the other kids. Kelvin had a particularly bad time with his mate Ricky who was laughing at him for weeks afterwards and to this day I have no idea how Ray reacted but you have got to admit that she had got a bloody nerve and was as brazen as hell.

Mam's relationship with Ray was beginning to show its faults and by now he was begging for her to stay with him and one day I witnessed him crying and pleading with her to let him stay but she wasn't having any of it and I watched him and his Pervy Father drive away in the blue Mini never to be seen again (another one bites the dust)! To be honest he was a total Wimp anyway and that was probably her problem with him, he didn't challenge her and she appeared to walk all over him. On reflection another thing that was odd about Ray was the fact that he didn't work but always seemed to wear the same sort of clothes everyday i.e. Black trousers, plain blue shirt and black tie and once when Dad visited I overheard Mam telling Dad that Ray was a Policeman and was just coming in off his shift, my arse was he! Dad, Kelvin and I always used to have a snigger about this latest plot and found the whole thing amusing as neither Dad nor Ray had an issue with each other it was just Mam trying to stir things up and see if she could either make Dad jealous or try and frighten him with the Law either way he didn't rise to the bait.

Kelvin and I settled down to life in the flat and we started to make friends. We were soon enrolled at the local Comprehensive School and even though the uniform for girls was black skirt and navy blue jumper Mam made me wear my old uniform from Warwickshire. Yes, not only was I the new girl who had started the first year three months later than everyone else but I was definitely the odd looking one too, this made me feel super self-conscious and if the truth be known I just wanted to crawl into a corner and be left alone as I found it extremely hard to cope with all the changes that were being made in such a short time. The school site was massive in my eyes and was also linked to the Council owned Leisure Centre of which there was a swimming pool and guess what ... I had to have swimming lessons in the baby pool where everyone could see me! I hated the swimming pool as well you know but soon made small but steady progress which resulted in me being able to swim a full width of the pool without cheating and putting my foot on the floor. There weren't many of us in the group as by now most kids could swim well before 12 years old and I vowed that if I ever had a child I would sign them up for swimming lessons as soon as possible. There was also a football pitch and long jump area which I soon became a regular visitor to, enjoying whatever sports and activities the school could offer. I still didn't enjoy swimming but managed the situation well once I was allowed to wear a nose clip and swimming goggles.

We eventually settled into life at the flat and took advantage of the grassed area to the front of the block where we had hours of fun playing football and other ball games as well as all the open space of the Park which had a Fishing Pool, Ski Centre, Children's Play Area and old Railway line that was surrounded by Woodland, this was much more the environment that we were used to and craved. Kelvin had his Best Friend Ricky who I mentioned earlier and they used to spend hours in Ricky and his Brother Ashley's bedroom playing Subbuteo and listening to rock music, their Mum Isla thought the world of my Brother and took him under her wing just like he was one of her own. I made friends with Sarah W and Sarah D who just lived across the road and we had some good times together. Sarah W's Parents were June and Brian and they also had Darren who was Kelvin's age and much later on Sally who appeared to be a mid-life surprise to all of the family particularly June. They were a nice family with June always staying at home and Brian who always used to be on the front of their property fixing their car. Sarah D lived with her Mum Cathy, twin Brother Jacob and younger Brothers Martin and Marcus, we used to have dens everywhere, at Sarah D's we used to hang out in her wooden shed and at Sarah W's we made a really good den in her brick outbuilding, where we totally cleaned it out and got rid of all the junk and cobwebs, we were soon able to put curtains up at the window, carpet the floor and put a mattress in there which meant that we were able to camp out overnight happy in the knowledge that we could secure the door as we had a key, it was really cosy and we were proud of our achievement. To finish off the den we had candles in there to provide us with light. I was terrified that we were going to knock them over and cause another fire but I have to say that we were extremely mindful of this potential hazard so much so, that we were super careful when we lit them making sure that we placed them immediately on some old china saucers that were going spare. We had so many good times together particularly if we had dared to go out during the early hours of the morning scrumping for apples or pears from the neighbouring Streets. Sometimes we would stay awake until 3am eating our haul or just talking about all sorts of things. Both Sarah's were really good friends to me and we never got into anything more than scrumping so I think that we must have been pretty good kids considering what other kids our age were getting up to.

So life ambled on and both Kelvin and I thought that it was a good idea moving back to Staffordshire to be nearer to our family mainly because we thought that Mam would calm down infront of the rest of our family and we could finally settle down to a less chaotic home environment but rather sadly and surprisingly this was not the case and Mam continued to conduct herself in much the same manner, still we were both totally shocked that our move didn't sway Mam to calm down but it was an enormous bonus for us that we were near our family as it was great being able to walk to Grandma and Granda's or over to Auntie Mays and Uncle Joe's house which was really handy if we wanted to escape from our home environment. By now I was spending a lot of time away from home over at my Auntie and Uncles and I began to dabble with food that I had never tried before, I was trying all sorts of things under the guidance of my Uncle Joe and was enjoying the experience apart from the day he asked me to try Lime Pickle yuk!

Now what can I tell you about my relationship with my Uncle Joe … Hmm I can only say that in my opinion me and my Uncle had a funny relationship to say the least. He would on the spur of the moment say things to me like "Ooh Karina your spots are bad today" Gee thanks Uncle Joe its not like I am feeling self-conscious or anything, you know with me being only 14 and growing up. God, my Auntie May still laughs about this to this day and I have to admit so do I but i won't tell him as I wouldn't want him to feel that he had been let off the hook so easily. Another thing that he would do which I have to say was rather annoying was when we would sit down at the dining table to eat a meal and part way through the meal he used to reach over the table with his fork and stab it into one of my lamb chops and take it for himself saying in the process "Ooh you didn't want that did you Karina"? Since then I have had a big issue with people taking food off another persons plate so much so that if it was to happen to me again even at my age now the 'Food Thief' would unfortunately be on the receiving end of having my fork stabbed into the back of their hand so BEWARE!.

While we are talking of food a local tradition of North Staffordshire is a type of pancake called an Oatcake; this is made from Oatmeal, Flour and Yeast and is cooked on a griddle. Oatcakes can be bought ready to eat with a hot filling: cheese, bacon, tomato, sausage, egg etc. or in batches of half a dozen to take home for you to fill yourself. My Uncle Joe introduced me to these when I was a Teenager and bacon and cheese is my absolute favourite, he also introduced me to Indian food which was mind blowing for me thirty odd years ago as the only take away I had ever eaten up to that point in my life was the more traditional Fish and Chips, Infact I'm not sure why people say that Fish and Chips are traditionally from the UK as they originate from Portugal Hmm another of life's mystery's. Anyway I got my first taste of Indian food when I tried a Biryani dish as they were less spicy and then I became a little more adventurous and worked my way up to mild curry dishes. I always thought that my Uncle Joe was so adventurous with his food and he didn't appear to me to be frightened of trying anything unlike myself and I have to say that I loved my Auntie May and Uncle Joe's Pantry so much as it always smelt amazing with the various spices that they stored in there alongside my Uncle Joe's homemade Pickled Onions which were divine as they were crunchy, hot and spicy tasting and were a perfect complement for the ever increasing Cheeses he used to buy. Personal food favourites of mine now are both Indian and Chinese food and I love to experiment with local foods when I am abroad and I have become a great lover of Seafood dishes including my all-time favourite French dishes Bouillabaisse and Plateau de Fruits de Mer.

By now Mam had also found her feet within the Community and was spending a lot of time in two of the local pubs called The Plough and The Woodcutters which were both close by, initially she had been socialising with our friend's Parents but it became obvious that she soon became a person to avoid particularly in the drink as she used to fall out with everyone and cause a load of trouble amongst the neighbours. Kelvin in the meantime was spending more and more of his time in the sanctuary of Ricky's house, choosing more often than not to stay there and sleep on the floor and I was spending more and more time at Auntie May's and Uncle Joe's. Sometimes I would just escape from the house and run to my Auntie and Uncles only to discover that when I arrived there they were out. I wouldn't return home though preferring instead to sit on their doorstep and wait for them sometimes the weather would be terrible but I would rather have sat there and waited than returned home. Sometimes I would sit there for anything up to three hours and only then would I reluctantly admit defeat and have to walk back home and back into the War Zone. By now Dad was able to call us on a regular basis as my Auntie and Uncle had had a telephone installed and as such I used to speak to him most Sunday evenings before I headed home ready to get my things prepared for school the next day, during our chats I hadn't the heart to tell him what was really going on at home although I knew that Dad would be well aware of what was going on with our Mam after all he knew better than anyone else and therefore knew what she was like to live with. It was also during this period that I met my best friend Polly and we became inseparable, I mentioned her briefly to you earlier, as it happens her Mum also had a drink problem and silly as it seems I used to find some comfort with the fact that we both knew what was going on in each other's lives and therefore had a real bond. Polly's Mum had what I would call baggage as her eldest Daughter Wenda was Fathered by Henry, then Polly's Mum and Dad split up and her Mum met a Black man who apparently died before their Daughter Amber was born. Sometime after this Polly's Parent's got back together again and had her, sadly this relationship second time around didn't work out either and when they split up for the final time Polly's Mum met a chap called Harold who I was led to believe was a married man, this affair resulted in the creation of an unplanned little Brother called Cameron, and there I was thinking that my life was complicated ...

Chapter 16

Disco Inferno –
(The Trammps)

We hadn't been living in the flat long when the most horrendous thing happened, I'm not sure where Kelvin and I were at the time but I remember that Mam was drunk and had been standing in front of the gas fire in our living room wearing just a nylon nightie. Somehow it caught fire and she soon became a human torch, it was obvious that she was going to panic, I mean who wouldn't in the same situation but instead of rolling herself on the ground she accelerated the flames by running outside and tearing around the grassed area attempting to put the flames out, it was horrendous to even think about let alone witness. She ended up completely naked and was badly burned on the inside of the upper part of her arm and on the outside of one of her thighs. The burns being so severe that they resembled rashers of bacon and she was hospitalised for about a week, I think. When Mam was discharged from hospital I had to clean and change the septic, puss covered dressings on a daily basis and soak and hand wash the used bandages, a task that absolutely sickened me. My pride was also hurt as the Neighbour's started referring to our Mam as 'Mad Alice' a name which still stands to this day, either way it wasn't long before the shame of her behaviour began eating away at me, so much so that I just didn't want to talk to her or be around her as she made my stomach feel like it was full of knots all the time and I just couldn't understand why she couldn't be like everyone else's Mum's.

Mam's love of drama combined with her trips to the Hospital via a ride in an Ambulance still continued as did her binge drinking routine which was always followed by three or four days of her recovering in bed feeling sorry for herself. Kelvin and I had to wait on her every need until the next time, which was never too far away. I by now had stopped taking the Parents Evening letters home from school as Mam had become too embarrassing to be seen with, life was hard enough at school without drawing more attention to myself with a daft Mam. I also didn't bother with any school trips apart from the annual Blackpool Trip as what was the point in asking her if I could go as the answer would be no anyway. I made this decision about the Parent's Evening after she arrived at one absolutely paralytic. She spent the entire evening slumped across the tables opposite my Teachers continuously sucking the life out of Polo Mints which she thought would disguise the smell of the booze on her breath. I was so embarrassed and vowed not to put myself through that again afterall school and home were two very separate places for me and that was how I wanted to keep it, instead I threw myself into sport choosing to be in every team going: I was Goalkeeper in both the Netball and Hockey teams, Bowler in the Rounder's team, in the Badminton team, Cross Country team and also the Volleyball team which meant only one thing ... I was barely in the house!

One night Mam invited Rosie and Daisy's Mum Ruby around to our flat for a drinking session, they lived next door to us and their Mum was also a big drinker. Sometime during the evening Ruby wanted to go home but our Mam wouldn't hear of it so when she decided to leave, Mam followed her out of the flat trying to make her stay and drink some more, this caused all sorts of commotion and once out of the flat Mam fell flat on her back on the grassed area of the green and couldn't get up again, so guess who had to be called? An Ambulance! Kelvin said that anyone else would have just got up and dusted themselves down but oh no not our Mam she made it into a big drama with another trip to the Hospital. I by now was wrestling with all kinds of thoughts about my Mam and struggled to see how after one of her drama's she could face people the day after as I am pretty confident that most people would have felt embarrassed or ashamed but no, nothing appeared to faze her.

I'm not sure how long we lived in the flat but it wasn't long and eventually we were on the move again after being offered a three bedroomed semi-detached house just around the corner from the flat in Church Hill Road. It had a really large rectangular shaped back garden which was surrounded by a six foot wall on one side and a low chain linked fence down the other side which separated our garden from our next door neighbours. The house was quite nice as it had very spacious rooms downstairs including the most enormous kitchen unlike the one in the flat and the other bonus being that we were situated even closer to the Park, the Cricket Club and our School, not to mention having our own bedrooms again and we were even closer to our school which was situated just across the main road near to the Park which had Tennis Courts, Cricket Pavilion and Children's Play Area and in my eyes was a really nice place to hang out in.

Mam's new Boyfriend was called Toby who Dad nicknamed "The Half Wit" he lived locally with his Mother in a tiny cottage alongside a fishing pool called Lower Lake which is situated next to the another park which also had a fishing pool. Apparently Toby was an only child and the story that I was told was that his Father had died when he was quite young and apparently his Granny more or less reared him after his rather eccentric Mother appeared to take little interest in him. Toby told me that it wasn't until he was 14 years old that he got his own bedroom, this was after an extension was built onto the rather damp and tiny one bedroomed cottage which was surrounded by mature trees and fields, before then he simply slept on the sofa in the living room next to the baby Grand Piano which completely dominated the tiny living room. The cottage was very cluttered and untidy with all kinds of things scattered all over the place and it appeared to me that Toby's Mother was oblivious to the chaos preferring instead to spend the majority of her time in the garden growing vegetables and attending to her free range chickens, which used to roam all over the place to the point where they would sometimes stray as far as the end of the Lane near to the housing estate.

Toby's Mother was also an odd ball in my eyes to the point of being aloof as she made no attempt to hide her contempt for my Mam. When I saw her out and about she would drive past me in her pale blue Morris Minor choosing to completely ignore me and I got the feeling that she thought that we weren't good enough for her or her Son to the point where I think she thought that Mam was after Toby for his money. Some considerable years later when Toby's Mother passed away I believe that he lost out on his inheritance after his Mother left her bungalow to her Sister rather than to him, to be honest I wasn't even sure that he had any money in the first place but his job with British Rail must have paid quite well as he worked as a Signal Man in the Signal Box in the town and had worked for the Railways since leaving school at 16, so I guess the pension pound signs were chinking in Mam's ears by now, in fact she was doing a good impersonation of Mary Ann Cotton as far as I was concerned. The story has it that Toby's first marriage had broken down within weeks of him saying his vows and as a result he had moved back to his Mother's which I am led to believe she was none too pleased about preferring instead her own company. Toby was an odd ball to say the least hence Dad's nickname, and he had the annoying habit of pointing his foot forward towards the ground similar to a Ballerina and constantly shaking his leg all the while rattling the loose change in his trouser pockets which made him look like a right numpty and quite honestly I was embarrassed to be seen with him so much so that I would not acknowledge the fact that he was officially my Stepfather. Now on reflection I think he probably had a learning difficulty that had escaped the attention of the school system. It was a shame really as I feel that you should also know at this time that Mam did nothing to help him improve his image as she used to cut his hair and it used to resemble what I would class as a 'Monk' haircut including the balding bit on the centre of his head plus he had a nose similar to the nose on Concorde so not exactly handsome if you get my drift.

I've gone off track again ... back to our new house which I was explaining to you earlier and which was so much bigger than the flat. Unfortunately because of the pecking order in our house I was allocated the Box room which Mam painted pink for me and guess what? Those bloody bunk beds and purple curtains also came with me. Kelvin had the second largest room that was painted a cool light blue and then Mam's room was lemon, and she spent the next few months really busy decorating and carpeting the place after securing a Social Security Grant to help out with the cost along with providing herself with extra funds for a few binge sessions. Kelvin and I continued to spend as little time as possible at home, although I do recall us having a good Christmas one year, that is since the Christmas some years earlier which we had with our Mam and Dad and our bikes, I don't mean materialistic wise, I mean being less chaotic with regards to being at home and in an environment without any violence and where Mam seemed to function reasonably well on a day to day basis. I distinctly remember that this was the year when I had a Digital Watch and a Ferguson black and white portable television and Kelvin had a Music Centre. Mam had come into some money in some way, not sure how but our presents were purchased from Eric Alcock's rather than her usual drunken jaunt around our local Market late on Christmas Eve, you see Market Day was a Tuesday and when it fell on the Eve she would get very drunk and then go and do the festive shopping. She was totally embarrassing and by now Christmas was a time of year that filled me with dread as it meant there was no reason to curb her drinking or behaviour as it was Christmas, you know the 'Season of Goodwill'! As it happens I have asked myself over and over again why I even bothered to get up on Christmas morning but at least I could give Kelvin his present and deliver the rest of my presents to the family. One year I rather excitedly said to him "Hurry up Kelvin and open your jumper"! Talk about giving the game away. Christmas morning for Kelvin and me would be a box of cheap Chocolates, His 'n' Hers Matey Bubble Bath and small box of Quality Street, which Kelvin one year rather sneakily had already opened (my box of course) and then after helping himself to some of the contents he then sellotaped the flap back down again, Slippers, Underwear and Socks and lots of Smellies from the Avon catalogue which Mam had bought over the year and as such one Christmas I opened seven Avon talcum powders! One particular year when I was 14 years old I had some mega socks NOT! I opened five pairs of white knee high socks that had Goofy, Pluto, and Mickey etc. up the full length side of the sock. What the hell did she buy these for I hear you ask yourself? Because Mammy Dearest in her intoxicated state thought that they looked like Roses! What did I do? I had no choice but to roll the socks down to try and conceal the print. It was either that or go without wearing any socks at all, yet another reason to have the kids at school take the mickey out of me. Kelvin will also tell you that Christmas Day wasn't about buying us things that we wanted, so it was pointless writing letters to Santa or writing a Christmas List as it was a case of Mam buying us things that we needed and so many times we have opened our presents only to discover a new pair of school shoes. One year she did a shocker when Kelvin opened one of his presents to discover a pair of fur lined shoes that only an Old Aged Pensioner would wear, all this did was hurt his feelings and reinforce the fact that we felt that she didn't give a shit about us.

Soon afterwards something went wrong with Toby's job and I think it had something to do with Mam visiting him when he was on his shift in the Signal Box and them having sex while he was on duty and as a result Mr Oddball was now on the rock 'n' roll dole. Mam had stuffed up once again by playing a major part in making him lose a really good job that he would have reaped the rewards of at retirement age when at least he could have enjoyed a comfortable life. I bet his Mother was hopping mad once she found out that he was out of work.

Life ambled on and one morning when I left the house at my usual 7am to go to Badminton practice I saw my friend Emma across the other side of the main road next to school and she beckoned for me to cross over. I didn't realise that there was a car travelling way too fast for me to make it over safely and I hit the car on the driver's side and tumbled across the windscreen finally reaching my ejection route on the opposite side of the car. I landed with an almighty thud on the road and lay there in a heap. By the time the Ambulance arrived I had been in and out of consciousness for some time but was becoming more and more aware of the pain I could feel all over my body. A crowd had gathered around me, some were Pupils from my school and some were Neighbours who had kindly tried to cover me up with blankets whilst trying to comfort me. After the Paramedics had checked me over they eventually put me into the back of the Ambulance and kept talking to me asking me questions, I guess this was to try and keep me conscious, "Where do you live"? They asked and I replied "Church Hill Road" and then one of the Ambulance men said "Don't worry, we can go and pick your Mum up first" on the way to the Hospital, Oh Boy do we really have to I wanted to reply! And so that is exactly what we did, much to my horror, the Ambulance Man knocked on the front door of our house and Kelvin answered the door eating a Lemon Curd sandwich. He calmly shouted Mam down out of bed and carried on getting himself ready for school not even bothering to ask how I was Tut!, sadly nothing fazed my Brother by now and by the time Mam got to me in the back of the Ambulance she was in a right old state, she was trying to take one of her heart tablets, totally going to pieces in the process. I felt that maybe it was her that should have been on the stretcher with me spectating either way we were both having a ride in an Ambulance. After a rather speedy ride to the Hospital I spent a fair few hours being checked out and observed, Toby arrived in between as it had been decided that he would follow us in the car, later on I was discharged with Concussion, two broken fingers and cuts and grazes, not bad considering that I had been in a fight with a metallic green Ford Cortina. Later on that day I was upset as I discovered that I had put a tiny dent in my new digital watch the one that I had been so chuffed to have had for Christmas. Once at home and I was settled on the settee and my Auntie May called over by pure chance with my little Cousin Lauren, and later in the evening the Driver of the car came to visit me too bearing gifts … a box of Milk Tray chocolates, he was shaken up too. The Police interviewed me and I was coached by Mam into saying that the Driver hadn't been speeding and in fact everything was entirely my fault … Bloody Liar! Even Zola Budd wouldn't have made it over the road the speed he was going and she broke the world record twice in three years in the 5,000 metres World Cross Country Championships, so I stood no chance, Zola by the way was an unusual athlete because she mainly trained and raced barefoot. Can you remember me telling you about running barefoot or in your pumps?

Now let's move on and I will tell you about two funny memories that come to mind from this house; the first being the time that both Kelvin and I got drunk when we were out with friends, we weren't together it was just pure coincidence that this happened at the same time. I had been at my friend Justine's house and we thought we would sample a few of the drinks that were in her Mum's Drinks Cabinet, we mixed loads and loads of different spirits together and got absolutely smashed, which was no wonder as I had never had booze before, well apart from the odd glass of Snowball at Grandma and Granda's. By the time I got home Kelvin had also turned up rather the worse for wear from having a few too many and we managed to get our own back on Mam a bit. We had her running backwards and forwards between each of our bedrooms with her trying to make us stay in bed, she wasn't cross with us which was a huge relief and I think Kelvin vomited but I didn't, I just had an attack of the giggles. The other funny memory was when Mam had made a Shepherd's Pie, which she had cooked and left on top of the cooker ready for teatime, SMASH! Oh my God! What the hell had happened, I've never seen her move so fast from the living room into the Kitchen only then to hear her cursing rather loudly. By the time I had made it into the kitchen she was well on her way out of the back door onto the front to see who the culprit was? It transpired that someone had decided to use the gable end of our house as a good place to put some cricket wickets and once in place they proceeded to fast bowl the rather hard, red cricket ball through the small kitchen window which was on the gable end and situated behind the cooker. Oh yes, the ball came to an abrupt rest in the middle of the Shepherd's Pie and Mam was hopping mad. It was worth missing tea for that night just to see her face, she was mega angry and on the war path to see who was going to pay for the damage to the window.

Another time I was invited to a party at my friend Dan's house and on the way Polly and I decided to call into the Off Licence in Unity Way. The lady who owned the shop was called Agnes and was really old, probably in her late eighties, she was a lovely lady and even though she smelt of wee and sometimes you could see dribble marks down her tights but all the same I liked going to see her as I wasn't sure if she had any family. The shop was always in a mess due I think to the fact that Agnes was old and couldn't manage the place on her own along with all the chores associated with running the business but everyone still used to shop as she always had some bargains on offer. Polly and I went halves and purchased a bottle of Cider between us and started to drink it on our way up the steep hill to Dan's house arriving roughly ten minutes later. As I knocked at his front door it was obvious that the party was well under way, the door opened and just as I was about to step over the threshold someone smashed a full bottle of Woodpecker Cider over my head knocking me clean out. I came around some time later lying flat on my back in the hallway with the vision of my Brother stepping over me on his way into the living room, thanks Brother for that, this party was wild to say the least! One of the things that I remember was a lad called Tod who I recognised from school was eating the soap powder out of a box of Daz Automatic, how could he stomach that? The other guests were playing "Guess the object" which once the person was blindfolded they had to guess what was in the bowl of Weetabix, Hmm my turn came and it really didn't take me long to guess that Dan had submerged his Penis in there yawn yawn! Why do boys do things like that?

Chapter 17

The Crystal Chandelier – (Charley Pride)

By now some time had passed and Mam was at War with yet another Neighbour. Dad always said that there wasn't a neighbour that she hadn't fallen out with and it seemed that things were not about to change. We lived next door to Silvia and her Boyfriend Murphy and Kelvin went to school with her eldest Son Andre, I went to school with her Daughter Melissa and their young Brother Justin who was younger than us and had just started in the First Year. Silvia was having none of it with our Mam and as such had started playing "The Crystal Chandelier" record over and over again well into the early hours of the morning to the point where neither me and Kelvin or Silvia's Kids were fit for school the next day due to the sleepless nights. The 'Battle of Wills' went on for a long time between Mam and Silvia and spread into a War that continued with car parking spaces at the front of the properties and a lot of unpleasantness in the back garden with Silvia resorting to launching her German Shepherds dog poo over into our back garden.

Kelvin recalls one particular day when Mam had returned home from The Woodcutter's definitely the worse for wear and trouble kicked off almost immediately with next door so Mam thinking that she was clever resorted to calling the Police and accusing Murphy of making her miscarry? Hmm this I found interesting as according to the letters that she had written to our Dad she had by now undergone at least seven hysterectomies! Kelvin said it was really embarrassing as all the Kids by now had listened to the rumours or witnessed different events involving Mam and was a good job that they were still willing to overlook these matters and continue to be our friends. Funny thing is that I think that Mam had met her match with Silvia who was clearly not going to be bossed around or back down from our Mam and as such when a three bedroomed house became available opposite Mam put her name down for a swap. The move was soon approved by the Housing Association and we moved all our belongings on foot from the old place to the new one. We now lived opposite our old neighbours and it more or less put an end to at least some of the shenanigans like the dog poo, car parking wars and loud music incidents. However, it didn't stop the two women from hurling abuse at one another or the sneering and sniping that went on if they were in The Plough or The Woodcutters at the same time. At least us Kids got on together, so much so that Andre was sitting on the front with me one day and asked me to show him my Fanny, was he insane? The deal was, he would show me his Cock and then I was supposed to show him my Fanny, so he went first and showed me his and when my turn came I point blank refused to show him mine, as if! I was hardly going to shit on my own doorstep so to speak by showing my own Brothers mate my private bits. Kelvin's other mate Darren wasn't any different, infact, I think he was far worse than Andre as at least he only propositioned me the once whereas Darren was like a Sex Maniac and, no Brother, before you ask nothing happened there either, God when I think about it you were friends with some weird boys.

Talking of bits, I wonder if Kelvin can remember a lad called Alex who lived up the street from us, he climbed up one of the small trees on the green that had a wooden stake supporting its trunk, unfortunately he slipped and basically hooked one of his testicles around the top of the stake and then plunged to the ground leaving a rather important part of his anatomy still on top of the wooden stake, needless to say he had a severe injury that required emergency surgery and a nice little stay in hospital, we cheered him up no end by taunting him with a song that we sang in his cul-de-sac, "Alex has only got one ball, the other ... "etc. We were rotten little sods and should have been ashamed of ourselves and our hurtful behaviour.

Mam had really overstepped the mark with her next drama ... Chakira and her family lived next door to Sarah D and we soon started hanging around together, she was from a really nice family who I think were either Pakistani or Indian and I think that her Dad was a Taxi Driver or Shopkeeper. Chakira's Dad used to drink at The Plough which is where Mam met him; anyway Mam called the Police to him one day after accusing him of molesting her? I can't tell you how much her accusation shook our community and it caused an angry tension on our little estate particularly as Chakira's Dad was devoted to his family and well respected within the community, he had never been accused of anything remotely like this before. I am led to believe that Mam pursued the incident and her case was heard in Court but unfortunately I'm not sure of the outcome however, I do know that the family soon moved away from the area and I'm not sure if Chakira's Parents marriage broke down, either way it was another pack of lies that Mam had fabricated in order to gain the sympathy vote only this time she really had gone too far destroying a man's reputation and tearing his family apart and as such I feel it is only fair to say that in my opinion my Mam should not have been "Crying Wolf" as we no longer believed that any of her dramas were true incidents as she had by now fabricated so many. Now you know why I said earlier that it was a good job that my Brother and I had established firm friendships as incidents like this in the past had lost us some friends, I guess it was hard for people not to tar us with the same brush even though it was plain to see that we had no control over our Mam, after all we were just kids but nevertheless it was hard at times for people not to judge us.

One day Polly and I came out of school and called in at the local Newsagents which was at the bottom of my road and situated just at the entrance to the Park that I mentioned earlier. I bought a local Newspaper and sniggered at the headlines in sheer nervousness "34 year old local Woman Attacked", I turned to Polly and said "I bet that's my Mam" and do you know what? It damn well was! I had no sooner got home and the house was buzzing yet again with the Police who had come to take a statement, God this was getting bloody boring by now, Mam was having more dramas than the TV programme Crossroads. It later transpired that this supposed drama had unfolded after Mam and Toby had gone to The Woodcutters for the evening and Mam had fallen out with him, she had then walked out of the pub in the huff and had taken a short cut through the alley ways behind the Fire Station leading to Birch Drive and this is where the "attack" had supposedly taken place. All the above had actually happened but on her way through the alley she had ripped her own black blouse and got herself into such a state just so she could make Toby feel guilty. Who knows what else she did while she was drunk and in that state of mind either way she should have been locked up for wasting police time as the Police did their usual thing and put an appeal out for witnesses including a photo fit of the supposed Sex Attacker. Mam kept her 'Trophy' of a Newspaper cutting under one of the cushions on the settee, now why did she do that? Kelvin by now had finished school and had been accepted onto a Painting and Decorating Apprenticeship with a local Company called Leech Brothers, he was settling down well into the role and gave me the opportunity to earn some pocket money by making his Bait every day and doing his ironing, this was great for me as we never had pocket money off Mam and it helped me out no end. Kelvin's new found financial freedom had a positive effect on him and the first thing he saved up for was a leather motorbike jacket which took him months to do but he finally managed to get enough money together so he could buy the jacket that all the kids were raving about at the time. Now for some reason our Mam was bragging to anyone who would listen to her that she had bought the jacket for Kelvin and we would often hear her saying "Look what I got Kelvin for Christmas", that was until Auntie May overheard her one day and said "No Alice" you didn't buy that for our Kelvin, he bought it himself, so you know what she did in response to her Sister? She put his beloved jacket into the dustbin just to be spiteful. Another time she took his trainers off him one day so that he couldn't go out of the house, she was really mean to us in lots of ways but I thought that she was really cruel when I started my Periods, as depending on what mood she was in with me was the difference between whether or not she bought me any Sanitary products that month. Can you believe it everyone else had a Mum that was really supporting their Daughter's through such a tough personal time in their life but no not her instead she turned this into a power thing as she knew it was difficult for me to buy these products myself as it was very often the case that I did not have any money and also I felt very much embarrassed trying to discuss my predicament with anyone else in the family. Mam had also stopped buying shampoo and was making us all wash our hair in washing up liquid, no wonder my hair used to look greasy and my Uncle Joe would often tackle me about the state of my hair which used to make me feel very self-conscious and it didn't stop there either because if we wanted to dry any clothes in the Tumble Dryer or have a bath she used to charge us 50 pence to either put the immersion heater on or the tumble dryer and many a time I have hand washed my clothing as she refused to do it if she was in a mood with me.

One year I was desperate for a pair of shoes for school and Mam came back from the local shops with a pair of brown, high wedge shoes which if you happen to know me, you would know that I would never in a million years consider wearing them and needless to say I was gutted particularly as she refused to exchange them for me, infact, on the few occasions where she did buy something for me I was bitterly disappointed, the shoes for example were like something an old lady would wear but with this daft wedge type heel. On reflection it appeared to me that Mam never seemed to give any thought to how her decisions would affect us and I had reached the stage where I was sick of having the mickey taken out of me at school and as such I developed the art of deflecting any negative attention away from me by becoming the Class Clown and making everyone laugh, this was also my way of coping with the shame I felt for my Mam. Memories ... like the time when my Auntie May bought me my first Bra which was from a Jumble Sale, infact this was the first of many items she bought for me to help me out, she also managed to buy me a genuine Harrington Bomber Jacket too which I was well impressed with. Uncle Joe by now was running his own Market Stall and selling plants and flowers etc. and he gave me a little part time job setting his Market Stall up on a Tuesday morning before school and after school I would help him to pack up at the end of Market day, he also gave me a Saturday job at another local Market. Funny thing is that when my Uncle first set up his Stall at our local Market the nearby Florist Shop put a photograph of my Uncle up in the Shop with Darts piercing through his head on the photograph, I suppose they saw him as competition but I just saw this as the shop behaving very unprofessionally and childish. My part time job had its moments I can tell you and my Uncle used to catch me out nearly every week with the dreaded cardboard. Hmm this was due to the fact that I used to collect all the pieces of cardboard squares up at the end of the day, these were the pieces that my Uncle used to write the prices of the bunches of flowers and shrubs on and then tuck them under the buckets of water or pots which was a great idea but my Uncle in his wisdom also used similar pieces of cardboard to cover up dog shit and barely a week would go by where I wouldn't end up with dog shit all under my finger nails Tut! My little market job was a great help to me and I welcomed both the responsibility and the extra money. My Auntie and Uncle were very generous, in return I used to Babysit for them so that they could go out for a drink with the family occasionally. My Auntie also taught me the art of plucking her eyebrows which she insisted we did on a weekly basis even though I hated this tedious chore as I had no interest in doing this whatsoever, all the same I used to do it as it was her time to close her eyes and relax. I spent such a lot of time with my Auntie and Uncle and it was great to just take off somewhere for the day resulting in some fabulous days out with my Cousin Lauren and then later with my Cousins Kris and Sam after they were born. We would make a lovely picnic up and take off on a Sunday morning for a day walking in Dovedale or around Chester Zoo; we used to laugh as we had barely got on the road when ten minutes into the journey my Uncle Joe would pull the car over to the side of the road ready for a sandwich. It was also during these times that I have precious memories of my Cousin Dionne coming to stay at my Auntie and Uncle's house for the Easter or summer holidays. These times were magic as we used to sit and play for hours and hours playing Gin Rummy and sometimes we used to be up until 1am with a big card rally going on. We had to be mindful to keep the correct scores as all the games would be added up at the end of the holiday and an overall Champion would be decided. I loved my Cousin Dionne and we were just the best of friends and we used to share everything even our secrets, well almost all of our secrets as I did not tell her what Elliott had done to me in previous years, I put this down to the fact that although I trusted Dionne with all my heart I was still trying to make sense of what had happened to me to the point where I still did not understand and therefore felt that because I didn't understand I couldn't explain to her what he had done to me.

Dionne used to tell me about her rather obsessive Boyfriend who was called Graham who came from a rather fortunate background where he appeared to have been completely over indulged by his Parents. At the time he drove a bottle green P6 Rover which even then must have been classed as a classic car, it was immaculate and very impressive and at the time all the young lads that were able to drive were driving ordinary cars unlike Graham's. He was completely besotted with my Cousin and went over the top with her to the point where he would randomly drive from Leicester to Staffordshire to 'surprise her' but she used to feel really annoyed about it as it felt like he didn't trust her and was infact checking up on her to see if she was two-timing him. He also had the worst case of Acne I have ever seen (his face looked like a Pizza) and I did wonder at one point what she saw in him as he wasn't good looking and didn't seem to have much going for him personality wise either infact he was just a spotty and lanky know it all as far as I was concerned.

My Uncle Joe always had a project on the go and as such he spotted a little wooden sailing boat for sale, he eagerly bought it and set about restoring it in his garage, he worked on it for a few months and did a really good job of renovating it and I can remember spending quite some time sanding the filler down where he had made a repair, he even took me to the Boat Builders yard to buy the Yacht Varnish and white Marine Paint in order to put the final touches to the boat and once finished it looked stunning. We had many a good day usually a Sunday sailing at a nearby Lake, mind you, once the wind got behind us it would be time to turn the boat around and sail back across as it was only a small lake. My Auntie used to sit at the side of the lake just watching with great amusement as my Uncle barked his orders at me, I was busy fretting about what was under the water as I never liked the weeds that grew up from the bottom of the lake, they looked like huge sprout plants and had all manner of things clinging to them. My Uncle sold the boat later and I can imagine that he made quite a tidy little profit from it, mind you he has always been good at making things and one day I was amazed as he bought all the materials to make his own Car Creeper, even down to upholstering the head rest on it, he had priced one up in the Argos catalogue and it cost £10 so he set about making quite a few and selling them on for just over half the price, thus still allowing him to make a tidy profit, they were as good as the ones advertised in the Argos catalogue.

Before we knew it Christmas was upon us yet again but this particular year Mam didn't do her usual last minute drunken shopping jaunt at the local market, oh no, this year she had something else planned ... Her wedding to Toby! I'm not really sure why but Kelvin and I were both against the idea and as a result he dug his heels in and said that he wasn't going to their wedding; I said that I wasn't bothered about going either but if Mam insisted then I wasn't prepared to go without him, so we decided between us that the best policy was just to get through the afternoon and keep everyone happy by getting the deed over and done with and so Mam and Toby were married later that day and were joined by a few family members and friends, strangely enough I think they either married in the Church where she had married my Dad back in 1964 or it was the Church next door to it, to be honest I can't even remember who came to the ceremony as it was of little interest to either Kelvin or me but what I do remember is my Brother wearing a new red and white Campri Ski jacket which Mam had bought him for Christmas and which she let him open early obviously to save her spending any money on a new outfit for the occasion, as it happens I inherited this jacket about two weeks after Christmas as it was too small for Kelvin anyway. Not long after the wedding Dad came to pick us both up and as he was parking the car up outside our house he was taken completely by surprise as Mam opened the door of the car and jumped into the front passenger seat and refused to get out. Dad by now was conscious that Toby was standing outside the car wondering what the hell was going on which meant that both of them were in the dark so to speak and after what seemed an age both men insisted that Mam got out of the car and that she stop making a fool of herself, but she locked the passenger door so that we could not open it to get her out. I was pleading with her to come out of the car before any more trouble was caused as I could see that this was not going to end well but my pleas fell on deaf ears, to be honest this wasn't the first time she had done this to Dad. Dad by the way could not believe his ears when she asked him to take her back! He was flabbergasted and had to point out the obvious, her new Husband who was standing only a couple of feet away from the car, she should have been ashamed of herself, which of course she wasn't, she just looked a total mess particularly as she was drunk again, bloody fool! As I said before this behaviour with Mam became a habit when Dad came to pick us up and drop us off again, even to the point where we couldn't get in the house on our return from the North-East and we used to have to ask Dad to drive us around to either The Plough or The Woodcutters so that we could try and track her down and collect a key from her. Some things never changed you see, of course she would be sozzled and it became obvious that Dad couldn't wait to get away from her which only made our farewells rather hurried almost to the point of being frantic which I found terribly upsetting as I hated Dad leaving me.

Life moved on and it was soon time for yet another dreaded family wedding, our Cousin Donya's ... where the usual happened, Mam was yet again sozzled at the Reception and came up with the hair brained idea to parade my little Cousin Lauren around to the rest of the wedding party along with her latest toy 'Dusty Bin'. Mam started pressurising family and friends to put money into the 'collection' which was being collected in my Granda's flat cap; this hair brained idea was supposedly for Lauren's pending holiday! God my Auntie May was so embarrassed and asked Mam to stop but of course she wouldn't, once this painfully embarrassing situation was complete she then went one step too far and got up on the stage and grabbed the microphone and started to put together some random speech which had nothing to do with the celebration, she was so drunk. My Uncle Derek and Auntie Margaret were fuming and trying not to alert people to their embarrassment but it was futile Mam was up there in lights that afternoon to the point where my Uncle Derek had to tell her that the Bar was closed! Hmm it was at this time that I noticed the way people looked at me and my Brother, it was a look I had not seen or maybe noticed before, the look of ... Pity. I can only guess that my Dad was also familiar to being on the receiving end of 'the look' too. Following Mam's Stage Act the celebrations finally ground to an abrupt halt and we managed to coax Mam away from the Reception and persuade her to go to Auntie Margaret's and Uncle Derek's house. It was surprisingly quiet on our arrival with Donya and her new Husband trying to make sense of what had happened to their very special day. Mam by now had started to feel hung over and asked if she could go and lie down upstairs, the bloody cheek of her, my Uncle Derek could not believe her request and was raging by now and said "No you can't, all the beds are taken"! This caused a massive row and Mam stomped out of the house in the huff. Kelvin in the meantime asked Auntie May and Uncle Joe if we could have a lift home with them and they said "Yes of course you can" but Mam insisted that we stayed with her, she was still going on about my Uncle Derek and HIS shitty attitude towards her! Rather abruptly Mam decided that we were heading to our old village and to Ned's house; he happened to be the best friend of Elliott and was also a Painter and Decorator. I still believe to this day that Mam had the visit planned all along and that's why she wouldn't let us go on ahead of her and get a lift home with our Auntie and Uncle.

It's hard to truly portray Mam as she was really vile at times and I don't think many people would stand up to her because if they did she would then make their lives hell. Some of the family took the tack that she wasn't their responsibility and would therefore stand back and let things run their course but for us it felt like she was our responsibility and anything that she did that was bad was our fault, of course I realise now that this wasn't the case and am amazed that both my Brother and I have impeccable manners and the upmost respect for people. I feel that this is amazing as kids learn most of their behaviour through their Parents therefore I count my blessings every day that Dad gave us so much positive input particularly during our early years.

Soon we were on the way to the village and Mam stopped on the way to buy a bottle of whisky which she drank the entire bottle of while we were at Ned's house, by now it was about 11pm and she was extremely drunk, Kelvin and I felt helpless and could do nothing to escape the situation and had to stay at Ned's and watch. As it happened it was clear to see that Ned didn't want Mam staying there overnight either and made it quite clear that he didn't so yet another row broke out and when it became clear to her that she was not going to win the argument and get her own way she feigned a heart attack which meant that Kelvin and I were bundled into the car and followed yet another Ambulance to the local Hospital. When we got there, Toby parked the car and left me and my Brother in it overnight until 6am the following morning, we sat a whole seven hours huddled together on the backseat of the car freezing with just Kelvin's leather motorbike jacket between us, which gladly he shared with me. It was so cold and quite scary parked up particularly with all the comings and goings that a Hospital brings, we didn't have a toilet to use and were busting by the time morning arrived. Mam and Toby on the other hand were lovely and warm having been inside the bloody Hospital all night and when she was discharged the following morning she said to us when she got in the car was "They wanted to keep me in but I told them I couldn't as I had my kids in the car" like we should have been bloody grateful that she had returned. Toby drove us to my Auntie Penny's house in silence where we were greeted with open arms, fed and watered and given the chance of sleeping in a warm bed which we gratefully accepted. My Brother said that he overheard our Auntie Penny saying to someone that she thought Mam looked like she needed a good wash! Later on in the afternoon instead of returning home and preparing to go to school on the Monday we headed straight back to the dreaded village yet again and to The Raven where Mam met up with Elliott. Kelvin thinks that the only reason she returned to the village was to save face after all the drama she had created the day before, all the same I was baffled as to how this was going to improve her reputation. On the return visit we also paid a visit to our Mam and Dads best friends Camilla and Connor who had always welcomed me and Kelvin with open arms but on this particular visit the reception was different, they kept us talking on the door step and wouldn't have us in the house, it was obvious to us that they were sick of Mam and didn't want her around them a minute more than they had to. It must have been hard for them to do that to us as they had always been fond of us but I understand why they did it.

I would love to say that the incident at the Hospital was an isolated incident; sadly this was not the case, as we spent many nights at the same hospital repeating similar Mammy Drama's but sometimes we were lucky enough to be taken into the Hospital overnight where at least we felt warm. It became a standing joke between Kelvin and me as Mam was in so often that we thought she must have her very own room and scoffed at the fact that she probably chose the wallpaper in the room too. Either way all drama's required a ride in an Ambulance, which would add to the drama and I was now beginning to strongly suspect that Mam was a Hypochondriac as she had either had an accident, felt unwell with her heart or had been beaten up, either way these trips initially made people feel sorry for her and gave her the attention that she seemed to crave so much, unfortunately people soon wised up to her and started to display signs of distaste to the point of avoiding us, particularly at family do's and it got to the point where my Brother could take no more and when some years later our Maternal Grandma passed away, he felt unable to attend the funeral due to Mam's behaviour. I think he was emotionally drained and felt that the only way to preserve his sanity was to stay away and avoid becoming embroiled in yet another drama, which I can totally relate to but Kelvin's self-preservation button was firmly pressed 'on' yet again and it broke his heart not to attend the funeral as it meant that he couldn't say his final farewell to our Grandma. Can you remember me telling you earlier about our Grandma and the Chapel of Rest story?

Chapter 18

Hanging on the Telephone – (Blondie)

Kelvin met a steady girl called Rebecca who stayed over now and again, one particular night I was asleep in bed when I was woken by the sound of Mam stomping across the landing and bursting into Kelvin's room where she then starting 'kicking off' at both of them. The screaming and shouting continued for what seemed an age but in reality must have only been a few minutes, the whole time Mam was ranting and raving at them and I couldn't make head nor tail of what the problem was. Nothing was going to stop Mam getting her point over whatever her point was and just before she left Kelvin's bedroom she turned aggressively on Rebecca and called her a Slut. Rebecca hadn't even spoken at this point but Mam carried on calling her all sorts of names before finally retreating back to her bedroom. A few minutes later Mam returned again for what appeared to be 'Round 2' and ordered them to get out of the f***ing house and don't f***ing come back. I was beside myself not knowing what to do for the best as I knew that Kelvin and Rebecca had nowhere to go, funny really when I think back as you might be thinking why didn't they go to one of the family but the truth was that neither of us would have ever considered knocking on any of our family's door at that time in the morning. I'm also fairly confident that Kelvin wouldn't have wanted to go to Rebecca's Parents house either as he wouldn't have wanted to explain to her Parents what had happened because let's face it in anyone else's eyes Mam's behaviour was crazy. It was 3am and as I looked out of my bedroom window I saw that the snow was coming down heavily and was leaving a thick, white carpet of snow in no time at all. I was too scared to leave my bedroom for fear of my Mam starting on me so I got back into bed and tried so hard to stop my body from shaking and crying as I heard my Brother and Rebecca leaving the house knowing that the only place they could go to was his car. Our Mam was never right in the head as far as I was concerned and I felt both disgusted and angry with her. This was not an isolated incident within our home as our Mam would take it in turns falling out with me one week, then Kelvin another week and then Toby, it was just a vicious circle and we just never knew where we were with her but knew who the target was as she would give each victim the silent treatment until she had got whatever it was out of her system. One afternoon she went too far after she took an ornamental sword off the wall in the Living Room and started hitting Kelvin with it while he was sitting on the settee, we were amazed but the funny thing was that the incident was so random and bizarre that my Brother laughed in her face whilst trying to put his arms up to shield himself, she had lost it for sure and of course she was sozzled at the time.

I think it was about this time that Kelvin got himself a nice little hobby of making Homebrew. I think he picked up some tips from our Uncle Joe who was very keen on home brewing and after some consultation he purchased all the equipment necessary which he sterilised to within an inch of its life and set about getting his first lot of Beer under way. Unbeknown to either of us, Mam was like a Kid in a Sweet Shop because when we were out of the house she must have been secretly drinking the brew, that is until I caught her one day scooping a mug into the brewing bucket before it was even ready to be bottled, she couldn't cover her tracks though as each time she scooped a mug out it left a scum like tide mark around the bucket. Who in their right mind would want to get sozzled on Bitter that hadn't fermented properly, she must have had guts like cast iron to drink it? She wasn't really good at hiding stuff anyway and one particular Friday I found a bottle of Bells Whisky inside the Tumble Dryer, one in Toby's Wardrobe, and one buried in the bottom of the dirty linen basket, Oh and even found one in the oven etc. etc. The house was full of her little hiding places, she must have thought that we were either blind or stupid or maybe both but it was clear to me who the stupid one was.

Also about this time Mam started taking a bucket to bed as she said she was getting up a lot during the night to go to the loo. Who in their right mind would want to wee in a plastic bucket when their bedroom was next door to the bathroom? I just found the whole idea disgusting and very embarrassing. During the daytime she was spending more and more time lying in bed with us all waiting on her. Toby by now had got another job as a Milkman after having quite a long time on the dole and life did not improve any, so much so that I didn't want to talk to him either and I used to get really annoyed when he attempted to strike up a conversation with me. Polly used to feel uncomfortable around him too, particularly when he used to mess with himself through his trouser pocket Ugh not another Weirdo! I think he was disgusting too, so much so that when Mam was on one, sometimes she was sick in the bucket and he would run his fingers through the vomit as if he was analysing it, totally unacceptable and thoroughly disgusting and the thought of this to this day makes me feel like I want to be sick.

By now I was fortunate enough to be invited over to Polly's Dads house every Friday evening where we would go to the

Chip Shop and hire a video for the night or sit and listen to Alison Moyet in her Dads red Ford Cortina Car which was really cool looking with its black vinyl roof. The next morning after we had eaten breakfast cereal with sterilised milk (Yuk)! we would go with her Dad to watch her elder Sister Amber play Hockey or we would go to the tile warehouse when her Dad was running the 'seconds' shop, here we would have great fun riding up and down the aisles on the pump trucks, using them similar to a scooter, lunch would be a Wright's Meat and Potato pie which was simply delicious and in the afternoon we used to get dropped off by her Dad at her Mum's house where we used to spend the day walking around the town or local Park, listening to music or watching a film with Amber if she was in a good mood. Amber appeared to be a bit of a loner and apart from the local Hockey Team she didn't really appear to have a social life preferring instead to have this habit of dying her hair a different colour every weekend and because of her mixed race origins she had a tight affro hair style which looked much better when she left her hair natural looking. Polly's Mum on the other hand used to send us down to the local Off Licence for a litre of Draught Sherry and after an afternoon of supping her way through this she would seem oblivious to the fact that Cameron who was about 4 years old by now needed some structure to his day e.g. a meal for tea, bath time and pyjama's before settling down for the night, he really must have felt unhappy as he always appeared to me to be really sad. I think it was lovely how Polly's Dad used to include Amber in our weekend sleepovers as he didn't have to because she wasn't actually his child but he must have felt it was important to keep the two Siblings together plus earlier in his life he had lived with Amber and had taken her on as if she was his own and I think that is amazing as he was a good Dad to her.

I came home from one of my weekend sleepovers and tried to open the front door of our house but something bulky was restricting it. It soon became apparent that the bulky object was infact Toby who was lying paralytic on the floor in the Hallway and his feet were preventing me from opening the door wide enough for me to squeeze through. I was so angry, I really don't know where the anger came from but I was really annoyed and I began shoving the door into his feet until I had gained momentum and soon found myself ramming the door harder and harder trying to shove him out of my way, this went on for some time until I finally admitted defeat and angrily retreated in tears of frustration and with a huge lump in my throat, I made my way on foot to the park so that I could try and calm myself down.

By now things were going from bad to worse and I felt that I had fallen into a huge, deep, black hole which had greedily swallowed me up because the girl Karina was lost not just to everyone else but more importantly to herself and with thoughts racing around in my head I found myself sitting on an embankment contemplating the meaning of life. I was 14 years old and had come to the conclusion that life was shit and I didn't want to live anymore. There didn't seem to be any end to the heartache and I was finding it incredibly difficult to cope, infact I was inconsolable as the realisation hit me that I was contemplating suicide by means of an overdose. By now I was wrestling with negative thoughts in my mind and massive physical changes as my body was well under way in the puberty department and as such I tried to hide my body by wearing trousers all the time and thick long sleeved tops, which when I think about it now my attire must have looked ridiculous in the sweltering heat of the summer holidays. When I returned to school after the holidays I found it traumatic to use the open communal showers as I didn't want to take my clothes off in front of anyone else. The other Girls just stripped off with not a care in the world for either Swimming or Physical Education lessons but not me instead I tried to maintain a level of privacy by undressing and dressing behind a big towel, this obviously didn't work when I was in the communal shower area and I used to run through it with my towel clutched in my hand high above my head preferring to give the huge shower area a wide berth and just get in and out of there as fast as I could. You see, I didn't like myself infact there was nothing that I felt good about and I think if I could describe myself as a teenager I would probably describe myself as surly because as sure as eggs are eggs I was certainly not a barrel of laughs.

I came in from school one day and asked Toby where Mam was and he said she had gone off somewhere on her own but he suspected she had headed towards the park which I have to say was a very odd thing for her to do as she was rarely going out of the house now claiming instead to be Agoraphobic (this was her latest illness), so I said I was going to look for her as I was feeling quite worried. I walked around the red ash track that surrounded the playing field and fishing pool area until I thought that I could see someone standing beside the water's edge, as I got closer I recognised Mam and she was wearing a blue dress and it wasn't until I got close enough to speak with her that I realised that she was very drunk and was slurring her words. Her make-up was all smudged around her eyes and she looked a right old state. As soon as she saw me she threatened that she was going to jump into the cold, murky waters of the pool so that she could drown herself which I thought was strange as she had always told me that she couldn't ever drown because she had been born with a Veil or "Caul" over her face, in other words she had been born with part of the amniotic sac covering her face. As it happens a birth with a Caul is rare, occurring in less than 1 in 80,000 births and a person born with a Caul over their face is supposedly born with the ability to see beyond the norm. This also works equally the other way and could have been seen that the person was a Witch, is this simply an Old Wives Tale from when they didn't know what the sac was? During Medieval times, women used to sell their saved Cauls to Sailors for huge sums of money because it was thought that the veil would protect them from evil or drowning and in order to preserve the veil, Parents were instructed to keep them in jars or containers with water in them, or by folding them in envelopes. My Grandma gave Mam hers when she became an adult and hers has been preserved in tissue paper which I believe she still has to this day. Other famous people born as veiled births include Albert Einstein, the Emperor of France, Napoleon Bonaparte and Charlemagne (Charles the Great).

Now getting back to the story, I'm not sure where I got the courage from but I told Mam to either jump in or get her back home because I wasn't prepared to stand there any longer and was leaving regardless of what she decided. I know that sounds really cruel or harsh but I suppose I was feeling quite short tempered by now and knew that she was only bluffing so rather than spend hours and hours trying to reason with her which is what I would usually have done, I just thought let's get on with it! Once I left she followed me home where the chaos continued in the confinements of the house much to my relief, as at least she wasn't going to show me up in public and I spent an early evening in the sanctuary of my bedroom listening to her carrying on downstairs.

The following morning I got up early and made my way downstairs into the kitchen where I took the axe head which we used to chop sticks for the Rayburn Fire out of the sink unit cupboard, I crouched on the floor and preceded to hit the back of my left hand with the opposite end to the blade where the wooden shaft should have been, attempting rather bizarrely to break all the bones in my hand ... Why I hear you ask yourself? What had I become? Was I attention seeking just like Mam? No, it wasn't that it was just that I felt the need to hurt myself or maybe it was a punishment for being so weak because quite honestly I didn't have the guts to swallow the bottle of Paracetamol that I had hidden away in my Dad's wardrobe, his wardrobe was the last object that I could still feel my Dad was still around, his wardrobe which at one time was his pride and joy with all of his trendy clothes from the Menswear shop Burtons was now in my bedroom. Every time I struck my hand the pain was excruciating and after I had done this four or five times the moment passed, I still do not know to this day how I didn't break anything but I can tell you it made my hand hurt like hell.

I had another use for another axe a short time afterwards, it was an ornamental one that we had acquired from when we lived with Ray and it used to hang on the living room wall along with the swords. I think I acquired it when Kelvin redecorated the living room and I hid it under my double bed. Oh by the way I think I may have failed to mention that by now I was in the middle sized bedroom and Kelvin was in the small bedroom. I'm not sure why we had swapped rooms but either way it was finally time for me to wave goodbye to those bloody bunk beds and say hello once again to the double bed that I was actually born in. I was woken up in the early hours of the morning with noises of Mam having sex in the next bedroom to mine with Toby; after quite some time of wrestling with my anger I lost my patience and shouted numerous times to "Shut up"! Of course the noise continued and by now I was trying to control my temper by saying to myself that if I hear them make one more noise I'm going to burst in there and bloody belt the pair of them, inside my head I gave them chance after chance but they still continued to the point where I lost it and got out of bed, picked the axe up from under the bed and stomped out of my room and into theirs, nothing in this world prepared me for the sight I was met with … Mam was sitting on top of Toby and was riding him like a jockey in the Grand National, she had no shame and as I burst into the room she turned towards me, all of her make-up was smudged and she looked a right mess, the sight was quite sobering for me even though I hadn't had a drink to the point where I retreated straight back to my room and Mam and Toby's brains remained intact, they will never know how close they came to having their *heeds caved in that night and much to my relief I didn't end up losing control but still the memory of that night is one that I will not forget, this was probably the closest I have ever come to losing control and one that I'm not very proud of, infact the whole incident still haunts me as apart from me losing my temper over the hoover and ramming the door into Toby's feet I would

---

* Heeds – Geordie word for heads.

consider myself to be quite mild mannered.. well considering the things that I had to put up with.

Dad called for our usual Sunday evening chat and let it slip that Mam had been calling him at all times of the day and night, she was yet again up to her old tricks of calling him when he had come in from a shift and was trying to sleep, he'd had years and years of Mrs Silent or Mrs Rant on the end of the telephone and she was becoming a nuisance as the whole situation started to get on his nerves, he said that he only wished he could do the same to her but of course he wouldn't because it would have prevented me and Kelvin getting any sleep so he just put up with it. The thing that I find really strange about this situation is the fact that Mam was trying to make Dad go to work without any sleep, so in essence she would have been taking the food out of her Bairns mouths if Dad had 'slept in' and therefore failed to turn up for his shift, was she really that short-sighted? After all Dad just wanted to take care of us as much as he could and the financial stability from him was a major factor in the part he wanted to play.

For me it was more the case that I was being woken at all hours of the night with one very drunken Mam blubbering on the telephone to the Samaritans, these calls lasted for hours and hours and plus she was always sozzled when she made the calls to them! She was one lost cause, I wouldn't have minded but the woman had everything that she ever wanted with Dad, she just couldn't see it until it was all gone and even then she spent most of her time in denial, she brought about her own misery through her jealous, twisted and sick mind and only had herself to blame. I cannot deny that she is the root cause for giving me such a huge hang up about saying "I Love You" as the only memory of her saying this is etched in my memory because she used to lie on the floor in the house in such a drunken state and cry for me to get out of bed and go to her, when I eventually did she used to force me to say those three little words to her while she gripped my arms tightly, this had such a profound effect on me particularly later in life with my

Husband as it hurt him greatly when I struggled to say those three very special words to him, after all, why would I? They were just words weren't they? The words that people say to one another during the good times but when the bad times come the very same people walk all over you just when you let your guard down; three words that can lure you into a false sense of security and when you have fallen as they say hook, line and sinker it gives them carte blanche to hurt you the most? My head was gone and my heart was all that I had left of my defences and I certainly wasn't going to concede this just for someone else to abuse me or have the green light to tread all over me, no, this was self-preservation after all I had such low self-esteem and my confidence was now at a super all-time low I needed to keep myself together and if that meant withdrawing into a world of my own at times then so be it.

During this time Toby's job as a Milkman was about to come to an abrupt end, the early morning starts were great for Mam because it meant that he could get his milk round done and then get back home to Mam about mid-morning, just in time to play Chauffeur to her or take her breakfast in bed! Then if she needed driving around anywhere in between her Agoraphobic episodes then he was at her beck and call, she as it happens had given driving up years before for reasons I do not know although the evidence could lead one to decide that maybe a drink drive charge was to blame although quite honestly I don't think that was the case as she drove one day and then just stopped the next without any warning at all saying that her nerves were playing her up. Although Toby's new job suited Mam during the week she was less keen however on him going out every Friday night to collect his Customer payments, so much so that sometimes she used to go with him and it was on one of these Friday nights that Grandma and Granda got vexed with her, you see Mam and Toby called into the Working Men's Club after they had finished collecting the money from his round and Mam put all the cash from the collection on the table in the Club. There were hundreds of pounds and Mam thought that she would be clever by counting the money infront of everyone; Grandma was extremely vexed and said that she shouldn't be doing it as it was a stupid thing to do as everyone could see all the money and they were rather stupidly leaving themselves wide open to being robbed but as usual Mam carried on doing her own thing choosing to ignore her Parents concerns. Not long afterwards Toby had an accident and crashed the Milk Float and we didn't half take the mickey out of him afterall the float was an electric one and only had two foot pedals, one the accelerator and the other the brake so how the heck had he lost control of it was beyond me? Then discrepancies with the collection of the money began to show, you know £5 here and £10 there which apparently led to the eventual sacking of Toby, it felt like the Dairy just wanted to get rid of him, so much so, he didn't have to serve any notice. Kelvin overheard Mam on the phone to the Management at the Dairy pleading with them not to take Toby to Court over the discrepancies all to no avail, so Mam failing to admit defeat then decided to play her 'Ace' card ... She told them that she had Cancer! Although the Dairy didn't appear to be too bothered with Mam and her Cancer, they did however, drop the Court proceedings, probably just so they could get rid of her too, of course the Cancer story was just made up.

It wasn't the only time that Mam played the Cancer game, oh no, she was bold enough to borrow money from a family member under false pretences saying that she had Cancer which of course was another one of her lies. The sad thing is though was the fact that she never made any attempt to pay back the money which is a real shame as the family member involved had worked hard to save, but not only that they had their own little family to look after so shame on her for stooping so low.

After I left the Sixth Form I set about finding a job and while I was doing this I had to sign on the dole (Unemployment Benefit), where I received the grand sum of £35 per fortnight of which Mam kept £25 for Board and Lodgings leaving me with the grand sum (NOT) of just £10 per fortnight to myself. I feel that it is worth pointing out to you that at this time it was hard to find work as UK Unemployment was at its highest recorded level in April 1984 at 11.9% (excluding the Great Depression) and even though the odds were stacking up against me I managed to secure my first job as a Recreation Leader with the Borough Council where I was based at the Town Hall but undertook most of my duties at the local Sports Centre which was the Leisure Centre that I mentioned earlier that was linked to my old School, all was going well with the job and although my contract was for only twenty hours per week the money was very good and life continued much the same.

Chapter 19

I ♡ ...

You know that I told you earlier that I would tell you the story about my Grandma and the Chapel of Rest well here goes ... Grandma had been feeling unwell for quite some months and her appetite had all but disappeared so much so that she could not face eating anything at all. She would not call the Doctor or allow anyone else to do so on her behalf as she was not a fan of Doctor's, infact she always used to say that she didn't want to cause any fuss. When she was due to take her medication which would help to ease her Rheumatoid Arthritis she always tried to take her tablets after eating an Arrowroot biscuit, she thought that by doing this it would put an adequate lining on her stomach for the tablets to sit on. Anyway an emergency soon presented itself in my Grandparents Bungalow one day, you see they had moved by now from the house in Gainsborough Road into a brand new purpose built one bedroomed bungalow which was Warden Controlled by a lovely lady called Evelyn, the downsize was much more manageable for both of my Grandparents and definitely made their lives much easier. One day the decision to call an Ambulance was made after my

Grandma became really unwell and she was rushed to Hospital where it was discovered that an Ulcer in her Stomach had burst, she immediately underwent emergency surgery that resulted in the removal of most of her stomach. A few days following the surgery it became clear that Grandma was not making any progress and she took a turn for the worse, the Medical Team attempted to stabilise her whilst they carried out further tests. In the meantime the family made a decision to take it in turns to stay overnight with Granda so that they could be on hand to drive him to the Hospital so that he could spend as much time with Grandma as possible especially as neither of my Grandparents had been apart from one another. Grandma's recovery was slow and she slept a lot but during the times she was awake she started to hallucinate, she was diagnosed with further complications which were thought to be due to a massive blood loss and which we have been led to believe led to Peritonitis, for those of you who are not familiar with this it is the inflammation of the Peritoneum which is the thin tissue that lines the inner wall of the abdomen and covers most of the abdominal organs, the result of an infection often due to the rupture of a hollow organ and which may occur in abdominal trauma which turned out to be the final stage of Grandma's post-operative condition. The situation failed to improve and our entire family were devastated to be told that Grandma would not recover and shortly afterwards she passed away in Hospital, which is sad in itself as she was always terrified of Hospitals for reasons I still do not know. No longer could we feel able to play the song "There's No One Quite like Grandma" which reached Number One of the UK Singles Chart for Christmas 1980 and was performed by St Winifred's Roman Catholic Primary School in Stockport. All the Grandchildren loved to sing along to this at our Grandma's house and as it happens one of the 7 year olds featured in the Choir is Sally Lindsay who went on to play the character of Shelley Unwin in my Grandma's favourite TV Soap Coronation Street. While we are talking of songs we loved the one that Benny Hill (Comedian) performed called The Fastest Milkman in the West because it always reminded us of our Granda.

This song was first shown on TV in 1970 and released as a successful recording, topping the UK Singles Chart in 1971 and reaching Number One for Christmas. Anyway back to the story ... my Granda had lost his Sweetheart and the family sank into a place where low mood tended to dominate over all of us and I found it extremely difficult to go to work or concentrate on anything other than my Grandparents. You see by now I had moved on from my role as a Recreation Leader and was now a Sports Coach with Port Vale Football Club which meant that I was travelling to the local schools to promote 'Football in the Community' and my Boss at the time was Alex Williams who was very understanding of my situation and supported me throughout this very difficult time. Alex by the way made 125 league appearances for Manchester City during 1980 – 1986; he also had a brief spell with Queen of the South and Port Vale, unfortunately Alex was forced into early retirement in 1987 at the age of 26 years due to a recurring back injury and this is how in July 1988 he returned to Port Vale and took on the role of Community Programme Officer until 1990, he left the Club in January 1990 to take up a similar role at Manchester City where in 2002 he received an MBE for Services to Young People Oops! Here I go again going off track ... Anyway after two weeks off work I felt able to return to the job that I loved and life moved painfully on without my Grandma, it was just awful to see my Granda trying to soldier on without her. Double Oops! I have done it again rambling on when really I meant to tell you about me and Kelvin ... you know when we visited Grandma in the Chapel of Rest, you see it was our first experience of seeing a dead person which was daunting to say the least and Granda had chosen a local Funeral Directors which just so happened to be operating the business from the terraced house that Reginald Mitchell was born in, you know the one I told you about earlier, the Designer of the Spitfire. Anyway the day arrived for us to say goodbye to our lovely little Grandma and off we went to the Funeral Parlour which was a trip that neither me nor my Brother were looking forward to as we just had no idea at all what to expect. The environment inside the property was not the best as we were led through the front of the house towards the rear of the property and into a tiny dingy room that had a sloping ceiling and was lit by a single red light bulb, neither of us realised it but our Grandma was lying in her coffin with the lid on which upset me greatly and the thought of the confined space really freaked me out especially as my thoughts wandered to the time when Grandma had accidentally locked herself into the outside nettie all those years ago. Once the coffin lid had been removed it struck me that it didn't really look like my Grandma, well I say that but I suppose it did but her nose looked different and it kind of threw my thoughts as I stood looking over her. When I tried to explain our visit to our Granda later that day he tried to comfort us by assuring us that there was no need for us to ever be frightened of Grandma as she had never hurt us when she was alive so she was hardly about to change and hurt us after her death which I guess made sense. When we left the Chapel of Rest Kelvin said something to me that I will never forget "Oh my God, I just almost shit myself in there", for a minute I thought that our Dad was there as this would be something that he would have said given the same circumstances plus when Kelvin uttered those words I felt empowered purely because my big, strong Brother was frightened just like me and for once I felt 'normal'. After this we made a pact that when it was Granda's time to go we would use a different Undertaker, as it happened we didn't need to worry about Granda for another two or three years as he soldiered on and tried to make the most of life without Grandma infact I think he was very brave indeed especially as he tried to focus on trying to stay strong for the rest of the family.

Grandma is buried in the local Church Yard and Granda had a heart-shaped headstone engraved with his affectionate name for her "Sweetheart" and without fail every Sunday afternoon we would visit her grave, me, Granda and Auntie May so that we could put fresh flowers on her grave, how my Grandma loved flowers so we always made sure that they were changed every week and that her little patch of ground was kept neat and fresh. Just before leaving the grave Granda would kiss the top of Grandma's headstone before all three of us would call into The Queens Head which stands on the opposite side to the Church and Granda would have half a pint of Bitter, I would have half a Lager and Lime and I think my Auntie would have either half a Shandy or the same tipple as me. When the time came for Granda to pass we made arrangements with the Co-operative Funeral Directors and as I had visited Grandma in the Chapel of Rest I did not feel that it was fair if I did not pay my respects to my Granda so off we went me and my Auntie May to see my wonderful, flat capped, whistling Granda (he was always whistling no matter where he was). I recall it was a very wet afternoon, bloody filthy weather infact and once we had arrived our mood lifted slightly as we were led into this very large beautiful room that had stained glass windows which allowed the light to flood in. We sat down on some blue upholstered chairs that were placed either side of my Granda who was laid out in his coffin in a beautiful pale blue coloured Shroud, at one point I recall swapping places with my Auntie and feeling quite upset as the side that I had moved to made me feel like my Granda looked different (it was his nose, the same thing that happened to me over Grandma when she was in the Chapel of Rest) to the point where I asked my Auntie to swap back with me. Anyway it just so happened that the door to the room that we were in was open and after about twenty minutes the strangest thing happened ... I caught sight of something out of the corner of my eye enter the room ... a very old, wet and bedraggled German Shepherd wandered in from the Street and started to sniff around the room, I held my breath for fear of the dog jumping up at my Granda and knocking him and his coffin of the trestle legs that were supporting him, I needn't have worried though as once the dog had had a good old sniff around he just lay down and settled on the floor beside my Granda to sleep.

I wonder if anything as bizarre as this has ever happened to you? My Granda would have loved this extra bit of entertainment as he was a huge dog lover and my Auntie and I let out a nervous laugh in sheer relief that a catastrophe had not been caused.

My Granda was finally laid to rest next to his Sweetheart (my Lovely little Grandma who used to cry with laughter and would then dab her tears away with one of her pretty little handkerchiefs) just as he had wished, "Together Again" he would always say.

Life moved on and by now I had met my future Husband and we started spending a lot of time together. I introduced him to the rest of the family before finally allowing him to meet my Mam. How I dreaded that day because to be brutally honest I was deeply ashamed of her and could never predict whether she was going to behave herself or not. After a couple of years together we thought it would be nice to go abroad for a holiday as I had never been abroad, infact I'd never even been to London so we got the holiday brochures together and finally settled on booking a fortnight in a place called Fanals in Lloret de Mar on the Costa Brava. Oh yes apparently this was the place to go especially if you were 18 years old. My Boyfriend said to leave it with him as he would look after me and although I felt the pending trip exciting I was also feeling cautious as I was leaving the Country for the first time and travelling to a place where everything was alien to me including the food, climate and language. The next few months flew by and finally the day that I had been looking forward to for so long finally arrived, we took a flight from Manchester Airport and landed in Gerona Airport at almost midnight, the July heat even at that time of night hit me immediately after we stepped off the plane, it was just like standing infront of a warm electric fan heater, we caught our connecting shuttle to the resort and off we went, via the town centre of Lloret which at the time resembled something similar to Blackpool in its heyday as far as I could see, it had a great big concrete channel which turned out to be the main sewer system running down the main street and on closer inspection I was appalled to see a dead black dog lying in it, Jeez! I was worried; where the hell had my Boyfriend brought me? Much to my relief we didn't stay there long, well just long enough to offload some fellow Holidaymakers and then we were soon back on the road and on our way to Fanals via a dual carriageway. This place was not doing anything in the way of impressing me with its scenery and after we finally arrived outside our hotel "Don Quixote" I was both relieved and lost for words, "Don Quixote" how original, for those of you that are not familiar with the name it is the story of 'The Ingenious Gentleman Don Quixote of La Mancha' which is a Spanish novel by Miguel de Cervantes Saavedra and follows the adventures of Alonso Quixano, who decides to revive Chivalry under the name Don Quixote.

We soon checked into our Hotel and went to our room which was on the third floor, by now we were long overdue some much needed sleep as it was 3am, our room was fine and would suit us perfectly for the next two weeks; further inspection revealed that we were on the side of the Hotel with our very own balcony so all was well. Next morning we awoke to the sound of rain, oh this was just getting better. Hmm I wasn't feeling this abroad business and couldn't understand why everyone raved about foreign holidays as my own conclusion at this point was that they were overrated. The rain eventually stopped and we sat on the balcony for a while planning what we were going to do on our first day, I looked around at our view to discover we were overlooking a Bar that had its very own Crazy Golf area, Hmm did this bode well? As it happens it did, we spent many evenings playing crazy golf with the added advantage of plenty of cold Spanish beers on offer we also enjoyed sitting in the outside area under the pergola that was draped with vines ... Mmm memories of ice cold San Miguel ... The first morning we planned to go to the beach to chill out and enjoy the glorious sun, I felt at peace with the world infact, I didn't realise it at the time but it was the first time that I felt content. On our way to the beach I enjoyed looking at the small Shops, Bars and Scenery along the way and was pleasantly surprised when I caught sight of the beach for the very first time, it was truly lovely and far superior to the beaches of North Wales or Blackpool, for starters the sand was a totally different colour being golden and fine in comparison, infact everything about it was different, the sea looked turquoise blue in colour and when up close it was crystal clear and it was then that I could understand why everyone had flocked to the beach and were having such a good time lazing around and then cooling off in the sea. Tranquillity did not last though ... as I was in no way prepared for the intense heat that radiated off the shingled sand, so much so that I resembled Zola Budd doing a 'run for it' into the sea as I attempted to walk sedately across the sand barefoot; this was something that my dear Boyfriend had failed to warn me about, I finally made it into the sea in record time considering that I had to zig zag through the sea of bodies that were blocking my pathway to the sea. After slowly edging my way out about four feet I took my next step which turned out to be another error as I suddenly dropped below the surface of the water and I found myself guzzling sea water in the midst of all the confusion ... I didn't realise that the Bay had shelf like drops under the water and a very frisky tide and so Crash, Bang, Wallop my elegant and sedately entrance onto the beach was ruined. I remember staying in the water for quite some time trying to soothe my burnt feet while my Boyfriend set up camp with the Parasol that we had hired and our beach towels spread neatly out over the sand, I spent the rest of the day reading one of my Catherine Cookson books (my Grandma first introduced me to these books when she gave me 'The Fifteen Streets' to read and I became hooked), listening to Bob Marley, John Denver and Don McLean on my Walkman and dozing for the first time ever in the glorious sun to the sound of the waves ... Heaven! Our first day was great and I really enjoyed relaxing. The following day I awoke to find that a layer of skin was peeling off the soles of my feet and my ankles were very red and swollen from the intense heat, still we settled into the holiday rather well spending alternate days at the beach and around the Hotel Swimming Pools. My Boyfriend developed a rash all over his skin which drove him crackers and he had to keep cooling himself off in the water, I recommended a trip to the Pharmacy and after explaining to the Assistant with a demonstration of my Boyfriend pretending to scratch himself all over she recommended a soothing cream in a yellow box which seemed to ease the condition almost immediately and later we were able to diagnose the rash as Prickly Heat. This tube of cream went everywhere with us on our holiday including the dinner table and it wasn't until we were on our return flight home that I noticed an advertisement in one of my Women's Magazines of the very same cream which turned out to be ... 'Lanacane Original Cream' ... Oh yes this amazing cream is used for the fast relief for itching and irritation of dry skin – external vaginal and anal itching Hmm nice! ... So glad that we displayed the box so proudly wherever we went NOT!

Another incident that I recall was when my Boyfriend had a minor mishap one evening after having a few too many beers, he decided to close the window in the corridor of our Hotel, I have no idea why he wanted to do this but all the same he did, unfortunately he didn't manage to grip the handle securely enough and the window came crashing in towards us and smashed! To make matters worse all the glass fell to the ground below and our only saving grace was that thankfully no-one was beneath thus avoiding serious injury, in the meantime I was trying to drag him along the corridor into our room before anyone discovered it was him, mission accomplished phew!

We also managed to incorporate a couple of day trips too, one of which was a Donkey Trek and the other a ride on a Glass Bottomed boat so I shall tell you firstly about the Donkey Trek which was quite entertaining as my Boyfriend had to ride on a white Ass which in comparison to a Donkey was quite some considerable size bigger. During the trek up the mountain it became obvious that the Ass was quite feisty and my Boyfriend had a hell of a time continually trying to rein it in but alas this was not to be as the Ass made one last final attempt to escape and bolted off taking my rather bewildered Boyfriend with it. After a rather nerve wracking ten minutes he returned to the rest of the group with the aid of the two Guides looking rather sweaty and flustered and with rather a tender bum and we were both so relieved when we reached our destination which was a run-down shack half way up the mountain, we couldn't wait to get off the bony backs of our furry friends and rest up with the aid of refreshments and I made the decision there and then not to repeat a trip like this again as by now my bum was also killing me after sitting on the donkeys rather bony back for the entire afternoon.

The second trip was on a Glass Bottomed boat and I have to admit was even worse than the Donkey Trek in my opinion as it appeared to be a total rip off financially as the boat itself was quite nice but it had a major flaw in that there was algae covering the glass in the bottom of the boat which meant that we saw very little of the marine life infact we saw more of the sea life simply by looking over the side of the boat. To add insult to injury the Crew took us quite far out to sea (I am sure that they did this so we couldn't escape their high pressure sales) and handed us some handmade flutes which they encouraged us to play and join in with the music and singing. The whole 'entertainment' was crap in my opinion and as such I did neither afterall why would I, I mean I got away with miming in School Assembly and Carol Singing so why they thought I was going to break into song in a foreign language and sing something that I had no idea of understanding of is anyone's guess, after ten minutes of frivolity the Crew rather craftily pressured all the Trippers including me into buying the bloody things, their selling tactics did not work on me as I firmly stood my ground and told them in no uncertain terms to "Away and Shite"! Despite my Boyfriends request to "Just buy the bloody thing"! Apart from this all in all our holiday was good and so too were the Hotel facilities including the swimming pool area and grounds which were all neat and tidy and pleasant to sit in, although I was quite surprised to see that some Holidaymakers were rather keen to hog the Sun loungers beside the pool so much so that they were up at ridiculous O'clock just to put a towel on whichever lounger they were going to commandeer for the day, this is where I heard for the first time other Holidaymakers complaining about 'the Germans'! Rumour had it that not only were they Sun lounger Hoggers but German women apparently had very hairy armpits and legs due to their aversion to shaving ... Jeez now that is truly scary and I spent the rest of my holiday averting my gaze away from anyone's armpits!

The Half Board food was terrible so much so that I have never booked a Half Board holiday since as the 'Starter' of soup looked very tempting at the beginning of the holiday but was sadly getting weaker and weaker as each night passed to the point that by the end of our first week it looked like someone had washed the pots in it and the breakfast? Well we just gave up on it and went to the local Mini Market instead to buy Philadelphia Cheese, Bread and Fruit as it just wasn't worth being in the breakfast stampede to receive what was on offer. Other than that we were having a good time and did the usual stuff that 18 year olds do by visiting Bars and Restaurants and enjoyed exploring the rest of the resort by foot. After exploring the local shops we bought the usual holiday gifts including a pair of matching "I Love Lloret" (the love bit being a red heart) airbeds, mine was lime green one side and yellow the other and my Boyfriends was blue one side and white the other, when everyone at home saw our holiday snaps with the airbeds they didn't half rib us for buying them, the other "His 'n' Hers" item we bought were matching Joe Cool vests, which are also on the photographs I am ashamed to say. One afternoon we hired a Pedalo down at the beach which at first was great as we went further and further out to sea but sadly this adventure was marred by the fact that I had my first experience of sea sickness, now I can hear you all scoffing at me but believe me it is true. You see I had no problem at all pedalling away out into the ocean, but after about an hour and a half of this and with our Cove just a minute dot in the distance I began to feel rather queasy, the sea began to look a peculiar shade of green and it soon became apparent that my sense of smell was quite acute as I could actually smell the sea, it was so intense the smell of salt, we tried to turn around as quickly as we could so that we could pedal quickly back to dry land but this seemed to take an absolute age and by now I was feeling really ill but still we persevered and finally when we made it back to dry land I wanted to kiss the sand beneath my feet and yes you guessed it ... never again!

With the holiday coming to an end it was time to pack up and head home to sunny Staffordshire. I was feeling rested as I had had two weeks of undisturbed sleep something that I had not had in years, I also had a glowing tan which made me feel so much better about myself, the black shadows under my eyes had disappeared too. I was chuffed that I had bought my first foreign holiday presents for the rest of the family and yes things appeared to be looking up! Alas it wasn't long before my optimism was crushed and as I played the homecoming over and over again in my mind I became really angry with myself for stupidly falling into the trap that life could become somewhat normal, how wrong could I be ...? You see all was going well until we parked the car up outside of my Mam's and I got out with my luggage, I approached the front of the house where I was met with the shock of yet another smashed door, someone had attempted a rather crude repair job by trying to cover the hole where the glass had been with some hardboard and to add insult to injury I couldn't bloody get in as someone had put the 'sneck' on the lock! I couldn't believe it. I had to go and search the local pubs finally managing to locate Mam in The Plough yet again sozzled at 11.30am; this was getting beyond a joke particularly as I was beginning to worry about lots of things particularly what state I would find the house in, my anxiety kicked back in as I wondered what my Boyfriends Parents would say because I was spending more and more time staying over at their house in the spare bedroom following one of Mams do's, you see she would either lock me out or throw me out, my future In-Laws must have thought we were quite a rough family, mind you who could have blamed them, afterall tongues wagged and my Mam never failed to play into the hands of all the local gossips.

Not long after my homecoming it became clear to me that Mams behaviour was not going to improve and our relationship hit crisis point as she got so drunk one night and threw me out and I had little choice but to walk the Streets for hours until my friend Celine who was also a neighbour and whom I had known since I was 12 years old offered me her settee for a few nights. Once there I vowed not to go back to Mam's ever again feeling that I had reached breaking point and quite honestly the top and bottom of it was that I could no longer take anymore. Obviously by now my Boyfriends family had become very aware of my diabolical home environment and as such my future Sister-in-Law introduced me to her Sister and Partner who by pure chance had just bought a place of their own nearby and as luck had it they had a spare bedroom which they said I was more than welcome to rent if I was desperate, was I ever! I eagerly accepted and borrowed a camp bed, sleeping bag and pillow and quickly moved in with a few of my belongings much to the relief of my Boyfriend and Friends. I soon settled in well at my new temporary home and tried to help out as much as I could with the household chores being mindful to respect my new Hosts privacy, they were out all day at work and I was out most of the time too so the arrangement suited us all and worked out great, infact I think it is fair to say that it was the tonic that I needed at the time as it gave me a chance to sleep soundly, gather my thoughts and finally settle my nerves down. Strangely enough at this point I cannot remember even telling my Dad that I was living in Lodgings as I didn't want to worry him, he would have been fraught if he had known so I delayed telling him anything until my next move ...

Chapter 20

The Pride

Dad had met a new Girlfriend called Petula who happened to live a short drive away from him, he seemed to spend quite a lot of time with her and her Son Tom, and we were soon introduced to each other on our next visit to the North-East. I wasn't quite sure what Petula did for a living, if she did anything at all, but her house always seemed chaotic with all sorts of things going on, for example, when I got engaged she asked me to go over to hers and choose an Engagement Present from an assortment of different gifts that she had in her house so when I next visited I chose a Duvet Set which I put away in my 'bottom drawer collection', a 'bottom drawer' by the way is a place where traditionally a woman might store clothes, linen and valuables in preparation for her marriage.

It soon became obvious to me and my Brother that Petula appeared to have quite a challenging personality and if I could avoid talking to her then I would as I only found her argumentative or difficult and after all Dad seemed quite happy with her so for the short time that I spent with her I just kept my feelings to myself as I thought that it wasn't worth upsetting my Dad. I think two or three years went by and very little had changed, thankfully it wasn't just me that was feeling this way about Petula as so did my Brother but like I said we didn't want to upset our Dad so we just made the best of things. I announced my Wedding Plans for the Summer of 1988 and found that Petula was being quite bossy and taking over seating arrangements etc. and involving herself in the finances of the wedding which to be fair had nothing to do with her as Dad and her didn't live together so there was no combined income or anything like that, anyway one day I had had enough and thought right! 'Good things come to those who wait' and I put my plan into action ... I waited months and months until finally the time came, and I only wish you could have seen her face when she arrived for the Wedding Reception and was looking for her name card on the 'Top Table', she would still be looking to this day if she thought that she had a right to sit with us, oh no I had great pleasure in seating her on a completely different table from us and to top it all Dad didn't even seem to notice that she was not sitting beside him (one nil to Karina)!!! I wouldn't usually have minded or have been so spiteful but for the fact that Petula just kept pushing and pushing until I had had enough, if she had been a little more respectful towards me I would have just let things run, rationalising that it was for only one day, but you see that was the problem as it was supposed to be my day and I didn't even feel like I was being selfish infact if I was to be honest I felt that it was ok for me to stand my ground for once in my life as all said and done it was MY big day and I don't think I can remember ever having had a 'special day' before.

The Big Day arrived and Dad was so proud of me; I can still see him waiting at the bottom of the stairs for me just before we were due to leave the house for the short trip up to the Church. His face a picture of happiness, pride and love all rolled into one when he saw me standing at the top of the stairs in my wedding dress, he took my hand and helped me down the stairs in my full length gown and veil and said that I looked beautiful and that he was proud to have me on the end of his arm, precious moments and memories for both of us. Everything was running to plan and although I was nervous it was clear to see that Dad was too which I feel awful to say but this made me feel better as at least I didn't feel like I was going through it alone, we set off in the Wedding Car ready for the 2pm Service, little did I know that I would cause Dad some major anxiety shortly afterwards because when we pulled up outside the Church I had this overwhelming feeling of panic so much so that I instructed the Chauffeur to drive on, all the while Dad was trying to conceal his panic and try and establish what the heck was going on, there was just one problem with that and that was that I didn't know what was going on and we ended up travelling quite a way down a country lane finally coming to a stop outside a beautiful row of terraced houses in a place called Dunkirk, was this an omen? Was I preparing for Battle? By now very little was said between Dad, me or the Chauffeur as we just sat there with the only movement coming intermittently from the Chauffeur's eyes looking into his rear view mirror at us. After a short time I instructed the Chauffeur to turn the car around and return to the Church where we had barely got over our nerves from this event when the next bizarre thing happened (I mean seriously you couldn't write this could you, but it's totally true) ... Dad helped me out of the car and we walked the short distance through the black wrought iron gates towards the thick wooden arched doors of the church where we both took a deep breath and I linked my arm through my Dad's arm ready to glide down the aisle when the unthinkable happened ... my deep breath had a knock on effect as the bloody zip on my dress went, oh yes the zip opened up completely all the way down to my waist revealing a full view of my back, bloody hell this surely must have been the second omen? Well a lot of hesitation, shuffling and scuffling followed when my friend Sharon who had helped to dress me rushed to the back of the Church to my side to try and assist, unfortunately on further inspection the only option available to us at this point was to pin the zip together as best as we could with the aid of the pins from the buttonholes! It was only after the ceremony had ended and we had signed the Register that we were able to examine the zip in more detail and after a few moments with the pins out were we able to readjust the zip so that it held the dress together independently, it appeared that the zip had initially been fastened together with some of the material getting caught up in it.

The Church where I married incidentally is the one where my Grandma is buried and the day after my wedding I felt great comfort in placing my wedding bouquet upon her grave, my Granda as it happened was too ill to attend the wedding, I think he also felt some guilt about attending as I know he felt bad about my Mam not being invited although he didn't put any pressure on me to reverse my decision as he knew full well the background into my decision.

Our Wedding Reception was held at the Civic Centre close by where we had a three course meal arranged for all of our Relatives and Friends during the day and a buffet for the evening celebrations. My family travelled from the North-East and Leicestershire to join in with the fun, I say fun as something quite bizarre happened at the Evening Reception, apart from my new Mother-in-Laws Best Friend slipping on some trifle on the dance floor and fracturing her wrist there was also the incident that my Brother had inadvertently become involved in ... it had been my friend Ellen's 40th birthday the day before and Celine had hired a Gorilla suit so that she could surprise Ellen at the party but unfortunately this plan had one major flaw and that was that Celine hadn't actually got anyone to wear the suit and this is where Kelvin comes in, Oh yes, Kelvin was going to rescue the situation by dressing up in the gorilla suit, so out he came onto the dance floor where he started dancing and cavorting around Ellen much to her surprise and pleasure, it was a great laugh especially as the whole drama was being captured on my wedding video, spirits were high and everyone was having a lovely time. Dad and I had been for a dance and we both took five minutes time out to stand back and admire the celebrations from the edge of the dance floor. Kelvin in the meantime was beginning to feel the heat through the furry suit as the combination of the suit and the summer weather started to get the better of him so he decided to unzip the suit halfway down and tie the top half of the suit around his waist so that he could attempt to cool down, in the meantime Dad and I were still in deep conversation discussing the day when we looked on in horror as my Husband of just a few hours sneaked up behind my Brother and quickly whipped the rest of the suit down taking with it his underpants revealing his bottom in all its glory for everyone to see and to make matters even worse the whole drama was being recorded on our video including the look on both mine and my Dads faces which I have to say was one of utter astonishment, this was definitely a video for 'You've been Framed'!

I know I told you a little about my Granda and his passing including the Chapel of Rest story but I would also like to share with you the rest of his story so here goes ... I hadn't been married long before I noticed that my Granda's health had started to deteriorate and after a few health checks, one of which included an appointment for a chest x-ray at the local Chest Clinic, I went along for morale support along with his eldest Daughter Auntie Margaret and youngest Daughter Auntie May. While we were there Granda was very upbeat and when I passed his cubicle in the corridor he gave me the 'thumbs up' to say that he was ok. I was on my way into the Consultants Room along with my Aunties and once in the privacy of his room we were given the devastating news that my Granda had terminal Lung Cancer, we were crushed by this news but were also told that Granda did not want to know what his results were so all three of us struggled to hold our composure when we met up with him; he was just his usual self but with one big difference ... He never touched a tab from that day on so I feel that he must have known that something very serious was wrong with him. His illness was a long one and his wishes were to be nursed at home, which we followed to the letter, by now I hadn't seen my Mam since she had kicked me out and I had gone into lodgings and a lot of things had happened to me since I had seen her including a decision I made in 1987 with my Fiancé to buy a little two bedroomed cottage which was close to my Granda and my In-Laws as I was married by now. I had reached the age of 21 years old and can honestly say that I hadn't had anything of a life, I'm not saying this for pity, no I'm just trying to portray to you that the road I had walked had been a rocky one and I hadn't been able to have the carefree upbringing that most other kids have, having said that my Brother was also feeling the same as me too. During this time I received a call to say that my Granda had been rushed into hospital, all I wanted to do was to be with him and after a rather frantic trip to the Hospital I came face to face with ... my Mam who was already sitting beside my Granda's bed, now I was faced with two choices: I either spoke to her and found out what was going on or I didn't. Now it would have made life very uncomfortable for my Granda if I hadn't have spoken to my Mam, he was already upset as she had not been invited to my wedding so I decided to put the past behind me and get on with things in the most positive way for my Granda. I have to say at this point I was shocked to discover that Mam was believe it or not amazing with Granda and helped to support the rest of the family who some of which lived away thus making it easier for them all to rally around and devise a realistic rota that would enable them all to nurse Granda when he was released from Hospital. This as it turned out played a major part in Granda's final weeks as it gave the family the opportunity to spend precious time with him in the comfort of his home just as he had wished. My Granda passed away peacefully at home with all five of his Children present and me, I was gutted as I loved him so much, both of my Grandparents were a massive loss not only to me but to the entire family and if I was honest after Granda had gone the family unit splintered afterwards, it was just like the family sticky plaster had gone as there was no longer any structure in place as everyone used to get together at my Grandparents home. It was during Granda's final moments before he passed away that we all thought he had taken his last breath only to realise after a few seconds which I have to say felt more like minutes that he gasped for air, me and my Auntie May rejoiced and clung to each other triumphantly in the fact that he hadn't really gone and this wonderful, beautiful person was still with us, I could have swung from the light shade I was so happy but unfortunately this feeling only lasted a few minutes after we realised Granda was truly gone.

Now lots and lots of stuff has happened both good and bad since losing my Granda for instance Kelvin is still with Rebecca, the girl who you may remember my Mam vented her anger on one snowy night. My Brother's life branched off in another direction when Rebecca's Mother, Father, two Brothers and Sister all emigrated to New Zealand. Rebecca was busy studying at the time on a Nursing course in Sheffield and Kelvin had started his own Painting and Decorating Company here in the UK, it must have been hard for Rebecca to deal with her family being so far away and eventually she travelled to New Zealand to visit them after they had settled. On her return to the UK she must have told my Brother that there were good opportunities and a good lifestyle to be had in New Zealand and I guess this is when they both made the decision to give it a go themselves and emigrate. It was soon time for Kelvin and Rebecca to depart the UK bound for New Zealand where they had arranged to stay with her family in their new home. Rebecca soon secured work and my Brother started his own business painting and decorating again and life seemed to be going well for them but for one major problem ... I think that my Brother was very homesick, I'm not sure how Rebecca was feeling but in the September of 1990 they both returned to the UK to temporarily live with me and my Husband in the little cottage that we had bought just a few years earlier. There were lots of changes ahead for me also as by now I was three months pregnant with my Son and I was by now working for my Auntie May and Uncle Joe in their business, Rebecca quickly secured a job with them too and life rolled on for a couple of months until either Kelvin or Rebecca or both of them felt the overwhelming need to return to New Zealand. Kelvin said that life was too bloody hard here, he couldn't cope with all the traffic and financially it was too expensive for them to try and build a home again together in the UK, he said that he felt like he was part of a rat race and that they had infact made a big mistake returning to the UK.

In December 1990 of the same year Kelvin and Rebecca decided to marry, I can't remember where they had the Ceremony but can remember that they held their Wedding Reception at the local pub which was a couple of doors away from my house and was called 'The Crown and Cushion' but affectionately known as 'The Pin Cushion'. The big day arrived and there was quite a gathering with Dad attending from the North-East, he as it happened had by now met his third Wife to be Joan and they were also married shortly afterwards in the January of 1991 when I was seven months pregnant, I should also mention that again Mam was not invited to my Brother's Wedding which meant that she had not seen either of her Children marry. Were we right in our decisions or do you think that we were cruel doing this? Both of us were not prepared to take the risk of having either of our special days ruined. After the wedding Kelvin and Rebecca spent a few days in the North-East as part of their Honeymoon before returning to New Zealand where they have both carved out very successful lives together and still live there today.

It has been so difficult telling my story and to be honest it has almost completely drained me at times but having said that it has also been therapeutic and a great release for me being able to share my story with you to the point where I feel a great weight lifting from my shoulders. There is just one thing that I regret throughout everything and that is that I didn't challenge my Mam about anything that she did to me or my Brother until she turned her attention on my child and then and only then did I stand up for myself and my Son. You see, I hated confrontation and would have done anything for a peaceful life as I hated all the screaming, shouting and upset and just wanted some calm in my life but still I should have voiced my feelings, instead I did nothing to challenge her, I was just a Kid you see and before I knew it the years had rolled on and the memories and bad thoughts just kept stacking up. Now before you go I feel this overwhelming need to share with you my final thoughts about my Mam afterall you have been there for me through everything now so that is what I will do if you can bear with me for just a little longer ...

Firstly my question to myself is 1. Do I love my Mam? Hmm that's a hard one isn't it afterall she did give me life BUT I think that if she died tomorrow I would like to think that it would just be another day to me, infact I have often wondered if I would cry? Maybe but they would not be tears of grief or sorrow, just tears from a child who wished that her Mam had been different, and to some degree tears of a chapter of my life finally coming to an end. What happened to the happy Mammy that saved all manner of cardboard boxes including toilet roll holders, cereal boxes just so that she could design, paint and create a little cardboard village for her little girl to play with? I remember that very special time when I thought that my Mammy was just so clever and the Bees Knees and I clutch at the memory of her holding me on the toilet when I was tiny as I was afraid that I would fall down the toilet and disappear for good, but in reality this feeling didn't seem to last and was replaced by feelings of a different kind, feelings that even today confuse the hell out of me.

Unfortunately my Mam used to scream at my Dad that she would dance on his grave, why? I didn't understand her anger or temper with him as he did nothing wrong to her, all he did was work hard to give us all a good life and was totally devoted to all three of us. We could have had such a good life together just the four of us if my Mam had just controlled herself as we had so much more than most people ever dreamed of, money in the bank, in fact when my Mam and Dad separated they had £900 saved, and Dad said that to put that into perspective the cost of a quality Victorian Terraced house with all the original features was only £2,200 to buy at the time. We were doing more than ok as we all had good health and I am certain that any decisions that affected our little family could have been discussed and worked out especially as my Mam was in the driving seat so to speak, I mean she was in control of how many children they would have to complete our family, Dad was happy to go with her decision on that. He totally adored her but it seems that she wasn't content with that and when the marriage was finally over; it appeared to all of us that she wanted to tread all over the memory, inflicting irreversible damage on all three of us, scarring us for life and I truly don't know why she did that to us and I guess I will never know why as it just seemed so senseless. Dad left Mam after discovering that she was having an affair with Fraser and I guess the rush and the excitement of this affair kicked the adrenaline in until she met Elliott and then just maybe she wasn't feeling quite so confident and maybe she had gone too far so much so that she felt that she could not undo all the wrongs and so never bothered to try and put things right? Instead Mam spent years trying to get Dad back because I truly believe that it wasn't until our escape from the village to the other side of the city that the penny finally dropped and she began to realise what she had thrown away and then she must have thought that she would just click her fingers and Dad would come running back, but I think it must have been a case of too little too late and instead he shocked her and didn't come back did he? Both Kelvin and I truly believe that our moonlight flit must have had the village celebrating; because by now they absolutely detested our Mam and couldn't wait to see the back of her, it wasn't anything personal to us after all we were not responsible for her actions but never the less the village must have breathed a sigh of relief.

Kelvin and I have since lost our beautiful Dad and I ask myself everyday why it had to be him? Why was it not HER, I don't feel at all guilty for even thinking this as it is the truth and I am sure you will understand my reasons, is that a really wicked thing of me to think? It's the truth though and I don't want you to think that I don't have bad thoughts about her because I do but they are all jumbled together now and I honestly feel that she doesn't deserve a life. Dad certainly didn't deserve to have his life cut short; he was a truly amazing person whom we will always love dearly. Kelvin and I will always hold on to the fact that the relationship we had with our Dad was truly amazing, but more importantly, it was genuine, we have always made him proud and he has always been there for us no matter what. You know what? It's a sad thing to say but I actually feel better to have been on the receiving end of all the pain that Mam inflicted upon us, because I would not be able to live with myself if I had done to someone else, what she has done to all of us, so you see I feel that both my Brother and I are in a far superior position to her as she has lost her two Children and her only Grandchild and that leaves her with nothing, is that her punishment? Mam's twisted and bitter mind has left her without any family; her sick mind knows no boundaries to the point where she cannot feel any shame in firstly disappointing her Parents and then her Siblings and in the meantime all she can do is keep writing her bitter letters because that's all she has left, just paper and ink.

Dad in the meantime had bought and paid for two properties in the North-East since leaving her and that was after starting all over again with nothing so I hope people don't ever think that she was the clever one because it is clear to see by everyone that she wasn't.

I couldn't protect myself from my Mam when I was a child but when I became a Mother myself and she tried to terrorise my Son in the same manner I put a stop to her after she allowed my 4 year old Son to watch the Horror film 'The Fly' which is certified as 18 years old, now that is just sick. She also frightened him at every opportunity with a wooden mask that was hanging on the wall in her Hallway and then she went a step too far the day a local Drug Dealer was stabbed to death in the flats that we used to live in in Westminster Avenue, my poor little boy told me that "the blood was the colour of my school sweatshirt and the knife was this long Mummy"! I had no choice but to stop her from damaging him too so I legally prevented her from having any contact with him until he was of an age where he could make his own decisions. My Son has been raised knowing that I was trying to protect him the best way that I could and I was trying to keep him safe, he was happy in the knowledge that when he reached 16 years of age he could make his own decision about seeing his Grandma, nothing has changed for him apart from the fact that he is now 23 years old and has no wish to have any contact with her. He just goes with the flow when he receives yet another cheque in the post that she has scribbled all over and the telephone conversations that she makes to him now and again. You see I openly admit to my Son when I get things wrong, after all, life is one long learning curve but the difference is that my Son always knows that I have his best interests at the forefront of my mind and is quite accepting of the fact that sometimes I get things wrong. He is happy in the knowledge that I love him more than life itself, and would give my all to him, in return he adores me and that is the best and most precious feeling in the world, something that I feel that my Mam has not felt from her own children since we were knee high to a Grasshopper. I will not be surprised if I receive any threats from my Mam surrounding this book but feel confident that at least I have the written evidence to support me with any potential legal action she thinks she can take. Anyone who has crossed her path will know that what I have told you is the truth, the whole truth and nothing but the truth and if you think about it logically we can't all be wrong about her now can we?

Saturday 5th July 2014

At the age of almost 47 years old I find myself travelling South on the M6 Motorway heading towards the village that I grew up in, almost 37 years have passed since I was wrenched overnight from everything I knew ...

On May 16th this year my Parents would have celebrated their 50th Wedding Anniversary that is, if things had been different ...

The journey is a strange one as I find my mind racing through my memory recalling so many different events both good and bad, I'm not scared, it's taken me all these years to overcome my fears but I have finally managed it.

Firstly I stop at Corley Services on the M6 motorway, the motorway that over three decades ago I was trying to rescue my cat Kitty from, I buy coffee and stand in the midday sun chatting with three of my closest friends as we eat our freshly prepared picnic, they are 100% behind me with the book and are all excited to read the final draft. On we go and before long I am turning the car right into Shakespeare Avenue where I pull over to the side of the road so that I can take a photograph of the street name, I then coast the car slowly down the road with my eyes darting in every direction trying to take in everything until they come to rest upon the house where my story began when I was only 2 years old. Further down the road past Bonnie's old house, my Auntie Penny's and Uncle Edwin's old place, Cleggy's old house until I reach the place where my little friend Maddie breathed her last breath. Before I turn right into my old cul-de-sac I bring the car to rest outside Mia and Jodie's old places, then I drive slowly into the cul-de-sac, turn the car around and park up outside my old neighbours house Camilla and Connor's, the cul-de-sac is so much smaller than I remember it, the only significant change is to my old house which has been extended quite significantly and appears to have swallowed up a huge part of the corner plot garden. I rush to show my friends the lamppost where we used to gather below for Bonfire Night and then I turn to take them to the Brook that Mowbray and I got into so much trouble in, it still has that smell, the corn is growing in the field, nothing has changed even to the point where I pick four Hazelnuts off the tree just at the edge of the field, they're not ready for eating yet but my discovery made me smile. We move onto the playing field that had the Tennis Courts, Caretakers house and white Pavilion, they are all gone only to be replaced by a huge brick modern looking Community Centre which covers much more land than the old one. I turn to look at the back of my old house; it is surrounded by six foot wooden fencing and beyond that is the big old Oak tree that still sits in the corner of the garden.

I am still excited and return to the car and make my way past my old friend Wendy's place on the right and then I am turning right at the top of the road heading towards the Park, but it's no longer there, instead a rough piece of land is all that remains, it looks like the local kids practice their BMX bike skills here. I feel so pleased that the Gulley's are still there, the one behind The Raven Pub is accessible so I walk through it in the hope that I can retrace my steps to my old school but the second one is all overgrown so I abort my plan. The Pub has gone and all that remains of the site is enclosed in six foot construction fencing that also surrounds the old Beer Garden and Car Park, although the metal frame where once the pub sign hung is intact the sign itself has long gone. Back in the car we head towards the Chip Shop, funny to think that the only Pub in the Village could not survive but the Village chippy has, I pull the car up to take photographs of the street name and a triangular warning sign "Arson Alert" catches my eye which is displayed at the side of the road, things have definitely gone downhill since I lived here and to be honest it is sad to see the village in such a dire state. It is like driving through a War Zone with the odd house that is well-presented looking like a sore thumb amongst the rest of the houses, if the windows on these houses could represent a face then they would look like weeping eyes reaching out to any onlooker.

I am still in a state of shock as I return to drive past Neil's old house and on towards Elliott's Parents house which looks shocking too, even the grass verges and greens are all overgrown and it instantly reflects the appearance that the village has been forgotten by all including the Council and it is not only hard to see but also to believe that anyone cares here. The red telephone box has long gone and has now been replaced by an open booth type steel one, the small Shopping Precinct that housed beautiful little shops that were a hive of activity now stand boarded up, the only shop that remains is the Post Office which still has the Post Box outside, this is so sad and yet so unbelievable. What do the villagers do now for a living now the Pit has gone? This place echoes poverty and depravation, it is everywhere you look, If Mam and Dad had still been together I feel that there is no way that we would have still been living here, infact I am certain that Dad would have got us out of the village and moved us to somewhere that was thriving. I continue to drive around the village and pay a visit to the Old Folks Home that I used to hang around and it seems to be the only place in the entire village that is cared for, this doesn't seem to have changed at all from when I was small. On I go to my old school which now includes a Surestart Centre, beside this a new housing estate has been built but it seems to have either been built on the old High School site or it has blocked access to it, either way I cannot find it. The final leg of my journey is the drive to Corley Rocks, the memories are flooding back and nothing appears to have changed here apart from the Council Signs that are placed randomly around the sight warning that Fly-tippers will be prosecuted.

My drive home is a whirr of my thoughts, the place is beyond awful, my Dad would have found it hard to believe and infact he would have been appalled, it is just like the life has been sucked out of the place and all that is left is hopelessness. One thing is for sure and that is that I will no longer feel the urge to go back there, it is nothing like the place that I so hurriedly left 37 years ago and I feel sorry for all the hardworking people and good families that have strived to keep a decent roof over their heads in the hope that they can look forward to a happy retirement because there is nothing but extreme poverty rippling through the place.

It's strange as I didn't see anyone I recognised today although I do appreciate that it has been such a long time but if anyone saw me and recognised me I apologise for my ignorance, I wish you well ... that is all but for one person who you all know who I am referring to.

For my Dad

1944 - 2012

It is with deep regret that I have to tell you that my wonderful Father sadly passed away at the young age of 68 years after an illness that he was immensely brave about. Unfortunately he never knew of my intention to write this book although we often laughed together about the fact that everyone has a story in them and sadly he will therefore not be able to read it, something that I am very sad about indeed as he would have been a great source of knowledge and his stories would have increased the length of this book no end, I am sure however that he is both pleased and proud that my Brother and I have put our heads together and created this from our memories in the hope that maybe we will finally find some peace in our lives.

I am proud to say that my Dad is very much a part of who I am and what I believe in, I have been privileged to spend 45 years with him and to be a part of his life, he taught me respect and good manners and I loved him for his dry sense of humour and because of this I realise with great pride that I am who I am because of my Dad. I will always love him and miss him greatly, he is the bravest person that I know; he fought his illness with great courage and determination always putting others first in order to try to lessen their pain. Dad I just want to let you know that you are always in my heart and therefore I am never alone.

Thank you Dad with all my heart for being my Hero, I love you Big Fella xxx

About the Author

The Author was born in 1967 in a Pit Village in Staffordshire and has one Son who is 23 years old. She enjoys spending time with her Family, Friends and her adorable Miniature Dachshund Poppy le Fleur. She remains close to her Brother who continues to share this journey with her and was so positive about this book that he wanted to know who was going to be playing his part in 'The Movie'!

This is the first book that she has written and reveals the people and experiences that have both influenced and affected her. This is her story of the highs and lows of her growing up in a Pit Village and her battle to tame her fears.

This book has been written in honour and loving memory of her beloved Dad (1944 - 2012) who would have loved this book.

Lightning Source UK Ltd.
Milton Keynes UK
UKOW04f2214221214

243556UK00003B/97/P

9 781496 998057